INSIDE**DELTA**FORCE

INSIDE**DELTA**FORCE
THE STORY OF AMERICA'S ELITE
COUNTERTERRORIST UNIT

FOUNDING MEMBER
ERIC L. HANEY
COMMAND SERGEANT MAJOR, USA (RET.)

DELACORTE PRESS

Published by
Delacorte Press
an imprint of
Random House Children's Books
a division of Random House, Inc.
New York

Visit us on the Web! www.randomhouse.com/teens
Educators and librarians, for a variety of teaching tools, visit us at
www.randomhouse.com/teachers

Library of Congress Cataloging-in-Publication Data
Haney, Eric L.
Inside Delta Force / Eric Haney.
p. cm.
ISBN 0-385-73251-1 (trade) — ISBN 0-385-90273-5 (glb)
1. United States. Army. Delta Force—History. 2. Haney, Eric L. 3. United States.
Army—Commando troops—History. 4. Terrorism—Prevention.
I. Title.
UA34.S64H36 2006
356'.167'0973—dc22
2004030945

The text of this book is set in 12-point Goudy.

Book design by Kenny Holcomb

Printed in the United States of America

January 2006

10 9 8 7 6 5 4 3 2 1

BVG

INTRODUCTION

It may surprise you to learn that terrorism isn't a new thing. In fact, terrorism has been around almost as long as warfare itself. Most often the weaker side in a conflict uses it; instead of huge armies and modern equipment, fear becomes the principal weapon against an opponent. Terrorism is theater. Fear gets attention, and it hurts. That's the point.

During the 1970s, the United States became the favorite target of any terrorist group worthy of being called one. America had become sick of warfare during Vietnam and was both unable and unwilling to strike back when terrorists hit American interests around the world. As the decade unfolded, the frequency and severity of terrorist assaults increased.

For years, famed Special Forces officer Colonel Charlie Beckwith had been the only one talking about the terrorist threat facing the nation, and what would be necessary to fight it. He had seen the need within the U.S. military for a compact, highly skilled, and versatile unit able to undertake and execute difficult and unusual special missions on a moment's notice.

Israel, long the subject of terrorist attacks by the Palestinians, had an elite strike force; Germany did also. Even the British had a commando organization, called the Special Air Service (SAS), similar to the one Colonel Beckwith had in mind. All of these units were what you might call surgical instruments—small, sharp, and precise—that could be sent at a moment's notice on missions that larger and less versatile units could not handle.

Colonel Beckwith's tenacity finally won the day and set into motion the wheels that would ultimately bring such a unit into existence in the United States. But creating that organization and bringing it to life within the rigid, hidebound hierarchy of the army wouldn't be easy. It would take men who were heroic in their own right to change the system from the inside out. I would be lucky enough to be a part of the founding of this organization.

Above my desk is a picture taken in 1982 of B Squadron, my old Delta unit. It is one of the few group photos ever taken within our organization. It shows a group of hardened Special Operations combat veterans still weary from the battle for Grenada. In the course of the next decade, nearly every man in that photo was wounded at least once, some multiple times. Many were maimed or crippled for life. And a number were killed in action. All of us carry the memories of those times, and all of us are better men for the experience.

For twenty years, I served America in the most demanding and dangerous units in the United States Army, as a combat infantryman, as a Ranger, and, ultimately, as a founding member and eight-year veteran of the army's supersecret counterterrorist arm, Delta Force.

In combat, I have learned that man is seen in absolutes—at his very best or his very worst. There are no in-betweens. No one has a place to hide.

War has also taught me that each one of us contains every ingredient of the human recipe. In war we are all by varying measure cowards and brave men, thieves and honest men, selfish and selfless men, weasels and lions. The only question is how much of each attribute we allow—or force—to dominate our being.

In life we are the same way. We will become what we make ourselves become.

In combat there are no winners. The victors just lose less than the vanquished. One side may impose its will on the other, but there is nothing noble or virtuous about the process. People are killed, homes and communities are destroyed, lives are shattered, families are broken apart and scattered—and only a few years later, we can barely remember why.

This is my story of that dangerous but fascinating world. I tell it from my point of view, as I saw it and lived it, and I tell it as honestly and faithfully as I can. I can do no more than that.

And in honor of my fallen comrades, I can do no less.

PART**ONE**

The Founding of
Delta Force

CHAPTER**ONE**

My story starts simply. I grew up in the mountains of north Georgia during the fifties and sixties. The area was part of the "third world" then, and some say it still is. Electricity didn't come to our home until I was a young boy. Indoor plumbing followed several years later.

I was the first of my family to graduate from high school, and we considered that a pretty big achievement, as our expectations weren't very high. It wasn't that my parents were against education; it was just that neither of them had gone further than elementary school, and they didn't have the ability or the understanding to help.

Though we might not have been scholars, we did know how to go into the military. I grew up listening to the war stories and tales of my family and friends, and I was determined to join as soon as I was able. I enlisted in the army in the spring of 1970, during the height of the Vietnam War. I was still in high school, and my reporting date was immediately after graduation.

I fell in love with the army as soon as I met it. The

military is a profession that brands itself on the soul and causes a person forever after to view the world through a unique set of mental filters. The more profound and intense the experience, the hotter the brand, and the deeper it is plunged. I was seared to the core of my being. I became a professional soldier, and that is what I will be until I die.

One thing I learned fast as a soldier is that armies hate change—and no one hates change more than the people who benefit most from the status quo. In this case, those were the general officers. But every now and then, there are generals who are innovative thinkers, and in the early 1970s, Colonel Beckwith's loud, persistent calls for a national counterterrorism force caught the attention of two such men: Generals Bob Kingston and Edwin "Shy" Meyer.

Kingston was stationed at Fort Bragg, North Carolina, and he readily saw the possibilities of the type of force Beckwith was proposing. But he also knew that getting the idea through army bureaucracy would be like dancing in a minefield—it could blow up at any moment. Pulling that off would take someone with lots of horsepower and a mastery of the military political system. Shy Meyer was that man.

In the early 1970s General Meyer was serving as the deputy chief of staff of the army, and rumor had it that he would soon become the chief. When Beckwith and Kingston floated their idea of a counterterrorism force to Meyer, they immediately realized that they had an ally. Meyer, too, had entertained ideas along the same line, and the three men enthusiastically shared their thoughts on the subject.

But first Delta had to come together on paper.

The men began by determining what types of missions their fictional unit would handle, because a mission is what dictates a unit's size. With that they were able to build a table of organization and equipment (TO&E), which outlines unit configuration, rank structure, and arms and equipment. The completed TO&E allowed them to forecast how much the unit's start-up and an average year of operation would cost.

General Meyer used his position in the Pentagon to start digging for places in the army's budget where the money and the men for the outfit could be found. After all, the army doesn't have men hanging around unemployed. Every unit has a manpower quota, and every soldier is assigned to a unit. But sometimes units that are alive on paper are not in existence at a particular time, and the men allocated to them are being used elsewhere. Meyer found enough of those to man their dream organization, and he uncovered a source of money to breathe life into it.

Next they spent months making sure their paper unit would be able to stand up to the scrutiny it would surely get. They had to anticipate every objection and prepare sound, well-thought-out answers to every question. When the more powerful generals realized that a new unit wouldn't intrude on their turf or take money from their budgets, they nodded their approval. It was time to present the plan.

The formal proposal for a national counterterrorism force was presented at the Fort Benning Infantry Conference in the summer of 1977. With all the details completed in advance, the proposal was approved and recommended to the army chief of staff for immediate action.

5

First Special Forces Operational Detachment–Delta was given official life on November 21, 1977, by order of Headquarters, Department of the Army. When Beckwith was chosen to command the new outfit, he immediately set to work. He handpicked a few staff members, found an old derelict building in an out-of-the-way spot on Fort Bragg, North Carolina, and started the struggle to bring the unit into existence.

It was not easy. In fact, it took several more months of planning, paperwork, and politics before Beckwith was even in the position to recruit men to try out for Selection, as the process of choosing operators would come to be called.

And that was where I came in.

The morning I was asked to try out for Delta, I was doing one of the things I love most in the world: jumping out of an airplane flying at 120 miles per hour. Life doesn't get much better than that.

* * *

> "C-One-Thirty rollin' down the strip,
> Airborne Ranger on a one-way trip.
> Mission unspoken, destination unknown,
> Airborne Ranger ain't never comin'
>   home!"

The C-130 transport plane bucked and shook side to side like a malevolent rodeo bull. *It's going to be a helluva ride till we can get out of this baby*, I thought as the big iron bird descended to jump altitude. Then the plane leveled off, and the bouncing and shivering, though still severe, took on a slightly more predictable tempo.

Now it was time. Barely able to move, encased in the weight of parachute, rucksack, equipment harness, and rifle, I lurched to my feet, hooked the parachute's static line to the overhead steel cable, and turned to face the forty other Rangers still seated on the red nylon benches that ran down the sides and center of the aircraft.

I was the jumpmaster. That meant the safety of all those men was my responsibility—a big job.

I looked at the Air Force loadmaster as he spoke into his microphone and watched for the red jump light to come on. Then, with a sudden whoosh followed by a deafening roar, he and his assistant slid the jump doors into the opened and ready position. Wind howled through the plane and whipped at my legs as I glanced at my assistant jumpmaster, Sergeant Allie Jones. He nodded that he was ready, and it began.

I looked down the line of expectant men seated in front of me, gave the fuselage floor a powerful stamp with my left foot, threw my arms into the air with my palms facing the men, and yelled at the top of my lungs, "Get ready!"

The men unbuckled their seat belts, focused their attention on my assistant and me on the other side of the plane, and sat upright in their seats, ready for the next command.

"Outboard personnel. Stand up!" I shouted as I pointed at the men seated against the skin of the aircraft. They struggled to their feet in spite of the wildly lurching plane, and when they were in line facing me, I continued the jump commands.

"Inboard personnel. Stand up!" I pointed with extended

7

arms at the men still seated on the centerline seats. With help from their standing comrades, they got to their feet, and the two groups formed a continuous line.

The plane was bouncing and rattling now, like an old truck hurtling over a washboard dirt road, and it was all the men could do to keep their balance. *I hope no one starts throwing up. If they do, it'll spread like wildfire, and the floors will be slippery and dangerous.* But this was a veteran bunch of jumpers and no one got airsick, even though the ride was getting worse now that we were on the jump run.

"Hook up!" I called, extending my arms high overhead and making crooks of my index fingers.

Only the first few men in line could hear the commands over the roaring blast coming through the open doors, but everyone could see the hand and arm signals of the jump commands, and it was a code they knew by heart. In unison the jumpers detached their static line clips from the top of their reserve parachutes, snapped them in place on the overhead steel cable running the length of the fuselage, and inserted the safety wire through the sliding lock.

I slid my fingers back and forth over imaginary steel cables. "Check static lines!"

Every man checked his own static line and then the line of the man in front of him. This was the crucial check; a fouled static line could kill a person.

I exaggeratedly patted the front of my chest with both hands. "Check equipment!"

Each Ranger checked his helmet, his reserve parachute, his rucksack and lowering line, and his weapon, making sure everything was securely and properly fastened.

I placed cupped hands behind my ears and shouted, "Sound off for equipment check!"

Beginning with the last man in the rear of the plane, the response came up the line, each Ranger slapping the butt of the man in front of him and yelling into his ear, "OK!" I heard the muffled reply faintly at first, but it gathered power and speed as the call rippled up the line, until the man directly in front of me threw out his hand with an OK signal, stamped his foot on the aluminum floor, and shouted, "All OK!"

Now I turned to the open jump door. I checked that my rucksack was securely tied to my upwind leg. Then I took a firm hold of the door frame with my right hand and ran my left hand down the other edge of the door, making sure there was no sharp edge that might cut a static line. Next I kicked the side locks of the jump platform and gave it a stomp with one foot to confirm that it was secure.

Satisfied that all was well with the door, I slid my legs forward, hooked my toes over the outer edge of the platform, and with a white-knuckled grip on the frame of the door, arched my back and shoved my entire body outside the plane to perform the first air safety check.

The 120-mile-per-hour wind tore at my clothes and equipment and tried to wrest the plane from my tenuous grasp, but I hung on with determination. I still had a job to perform, and we were miles short of the drop zone (DZ).

First I looked forward to orient myself, and then I checked for the positions of the other planes. I looked up to make sure no one was above us, then toward the rear to make certain no one was back there. We were the last plane in the flight, and I was glad to see the other birds all in their proper positions. I tilted my head down just a bit so that the brim of my helmet cut the wind from my eyes; then I concentrated on the ground ahead, looking for the checkpoints that told me we were approaching Fort Stewart, Georgia, and Taylor's Creek Drop Zone.

In the distance ahead, I caught sight of the huge DZ, a rectangular slab of white sand and scrub brush in an endless green forest. I watched its steady approach, and then, when it was just in front of the plane's nose, I wrenched myself back inside, pointed to the open doorway, and shouted to the first man in line the phrase that thrills every paratrooper: "Stand in the door!"

The human energy in the plane crackled as the soldier threw his static line into my waiting hand, put his feet on the jump platform, and grasped the outside of the shuddering door frame. Knees cocked like levers, arms tensed, he looked with steady eyes straight out the wind-blasted and howling door, waiting for the ultimate command. An eighteen-year-old private first class, Ricky Magee was the youngest jumper in the plane, but he was showing the steady courage of an old hand.

I held him by his parachute harness and looked around his chest as the drop zone slid under the belly of the plane. I looked back inside just in time to see the red light extinguish and the green light come on in its place.

It was as if a switch had been thrown. My right arm felt electric as I swung it sharply forward, gave the jumper a stinging slap low on the back of his thigh, and yelled into his ear, "Go!"

He sprang out the door as if he'd been shot from an automatic cannon, while behind him a human conveyor belt of fresh ammo rushed for the breach of the exit door.

Slap, "Go!" Slap, "Go!" Slap, "Go!"

The rapidly shortening line of men disappeared from sight as the wildly lunging plane, a thousand feet above the ground, disgorged its human cargo into the ether. *Like Jonahs from the belly of the whale.* As the last man hurled himself into space, I looked out the plane and down at the descending jumpers to make sure no one was hung up on the plane and being dragged to his death.

Satisfied that all was OK, I looked at my assistant, who had been doing the same thing in the other doorway. He shouted across to me, "Clear to the rear!"

I gave him a thumbs-up and answered, "Clear!" then pointed at him and yelled, "Go!"

He turned to the door, hesitated the split second he needed to take a good door position, then launched himself from view. I quickly checked outside and below to see that he had a chute over his head, glanced at the still-green jump light, and rocketed myself out the door into the full blast of the air.

Tight body position. Feet and knees pressed together, hands grasping the ends of the reserve chute, head down with chin tucked into chest, and count.

One thousand! Two thousand! A hard tug at my back as the parachute was jerked from its pack. *Three thousand!* The drag of the elongated but still unopened chute acted as an air brake, immediately slowing my forward movement, tilting my back toward the earth, and I watched as the tail of the plane sailed past over the tips of my boots.

Four thousand! A full parachute. Feet once again pointed toward the ground, I checked the canopy. It looked good. No tears in the green fabric and no lines out of place. *And after the overwhelming noise inside the airplane, the world is suddenly silent.*

I grabbed the handles of the control lines and pulled them down to the level of my helmet as I quickly looked all around for other jumpers. *Ah, plenty of clear air.* I checked for the direction of smoke on the drop zone, then let the parachute fly so that I could also gauge the direction of the wind up here. I let the canopy run with the wind; I was a long way from the assembly point and I wanted the parachute to take me as close as it possibly could.

Two hundred feet above the ground, I bent my knees so that my rucksack would have a ramp to slide off. I reached down and pulled the quick-release tabs to the rucksack and felt it drop free until it hit the end of the twenty-foot lowering line with a yank. The tall Georgia pines at the side of the drop zone drifted lazily upward, and when I was level with their tops, I faced the canopy into the wind and prepared to land.

Shove the rifle over so that it's not under my armpit or it'll bend the barrel and dislocate my shoulder when I hit the ground. Legs slightly bent, feet and knees together, elbows in front of the face, hands even with the top of the helmet . . . and relax. The ground came hurtling upward with amazing speed, and the rucksack hit with a solid *thunk. Relax, relax, relax . . .*

At a speed of twenty-two feet per second, I made jolting impact with the earth. Balls of the feet, calves, sides of the thighs, butt, and back of the shoulders made contact in a practiced rolling sequence that spread the energy of the controlled crash across the length of my body. I heard, as if from a distance, the thump and jangle of equipment as my load and I completed our short flight and sudden landing. And then it was over.

Everything still works. And any parachute landing is a good one if you can get up and walk away. I came to rest, shucked myself of the harness, and ran to the canopy to fold and stow it away before a puff of wind could inflate it again. I quickly stuffed my chute into its kit bag, donned my gear, and set out at a fast trot to rejoin my company.

That day we had a rare and unexpected treat. Following an exercise, we usually road-marched the twenty miles from the drop zone back to the barracks. But we were returning from a long and arduous month in the jungles of Panama and we had a lot of work ahead of us, cleaning and turning in weapons and equipment, so the colonel had us trucked back to camp instead.

Four hours later everything was accounted for and back in its proper place. The formation came to attention, the first sergeant called, "Dismissed!" and with a thundering *"Hoo-ah!"* the 158 men of Charlie Company, First Ranger Battalion, were released for a well-deserved three-day weekend.

I watched my platoon as it immediately disintegrated into individuals and small groups of buddies. I was about to walk away when Glen Morrell, the battalion command sergeant major, called me to his side.

"Sergeant Haney, I want you to report to the battalion conference room and meet someone who'd like to speak with you."

"Certainly, Sergeant Major," I said. "Who is it?"

"He's an old friend of mine, and I think you'll find what he has to say pretty interesting," he replied with the lop-sided smile that habitually adorned his rugged face. "He's waiting for you now."

"Wilco, Sergeant Major. I'm on my way." And with a salute I moved out sharply in the direction of battalion headquarters.

I thought the world of Sergeant Major Morrell. He was one of the very finest leaders I had ever known. A practical yet deeply thoughtful man, he was that rare combination of action and intellect.

Morrell had come to us the previous year, after our former sergeant major, Henry Caro, had been killed on a para-chute jump. With the battalion's reputation as a hardship posting, no other sergeant major in the army would join us. When Morrell heard that no Ranger-qualified sergeant major would accept the assignment, he volunteered and, at age forty-two, attended Ranger School so that he could accept the posting as command sergeant major. He was as hard as woodpecker lips, and he had my utter respect. If he had wanted me to meet Beelzebub himself, I would have been confident it was all for the best.

The meeting in the conference room turned out to be an interview to attend tryouts for a secretive new unit that was forming at Fort Bragg—the one we had been hearing rumors about. The man I spoke with was tall and broad-shouldered, with well-combed dark hair, penetrating brown eyes, and a hint of a tin-roof twang in his quiet, intelligent voice. He was dressed in civvies, never gave his name, and

14

told me nearly nothing about his organization. I later came to know him as Sergeant Major William "Country" Grimes, the man handpicked by Colonel Charlie Beckwith to be his sergeant major.

He had my personnel records open on the table in front of him, and he glanced at them occasionally as we talked about my career, about the units I had been in and the assignments I had held. He told me that this was a chance to be a charter member of a unit that would be unique in the American military—the nation's first unit dedicated to fighting international terrorism.

The prerequisites to try out were: Minimum age of twenty-two. Minimum time in service of four years and two months. Minimum rank of staff sergeant. Pass a hundred-meter swim test while wearing boots and fatigues, and pass the Ranger/Special Forces PT (physical training) test. Have a minimum score of 110 on the army general aptitude test, no court-martial convictions, and no record of recurring disciplinary problems.

About the only other thing Grimes told me was that if I was accepted, I could expect hard work, plenty of danger, and no recognition.

I had been thinking a great deal lately about what I wanted to do after my assignment with the Rangers. I didn't know whether I wanted to go overseas again or into Special Forces. I was positive of one thing: I didn't want to be detailed as an instructor at a school somewhere. But since I had just been picked up for promotion to sergeant first class and had never had a nontactical assignment, that was a distinct possibility. I had a fair number of options, but none sounded as good as what I had just heard. Given all this, I signed up on the spot.

Grimes told me to expect orders soon to go to Fort Bragg for about a month. He gave me a phone number to call if I had any questions or changed my mind about going. And that was it. Just a few weeks later, I received orders directing me to report to Moon Hall at Fort Bragg on or about noon, September 13, 1978.

Forming a brand-new outfit and creating new operating methods is a noncommissioned officer's dream come true, but still, I was apprehensive. There was a lot of unknown here, not the least of which was what I would do if I failed to make it through the selection program. I had turned my platoon over to Tom Duke, the new platoon sergeant. Duke was a solid, experienced leader who had been with us for a year. I had come to know and respect him in that time, so I knew that the men would be in good hands no matter what. As it became known that I was going to Fort Bragg, my troops wished me well and told me, "If anyone can make it into that new unit, you can, Sergeant Haney." Man, they were going to be a hard bunch to face if I came back a failure.

In my favor, I had been in the army for eight years. I was a seasoned and experienced infantryman. I had successfully completed two of the hardest courses in the military— Ranger School and the jumpmaster course. I had been a platoon sergeant for more than four years, with the last two of those years in the Rangers.

Life in the Rangers was austere. In fact, it was downright severe. If there were two ways of accomplishing a given task, we always took the hard way. We never took shortcuts and we never spared any effort. We spent at least three weeks of every month in the field, and we deployed on extended training to the Arctic, the desert, and the jungle three times a year. We were also subject to two "no-notice" exercises annually and participated in major army or NATO programs every year.

Life in the Rangers was so difficult that most men failed to complete a full two-year tour with the unit, and numerous injuries also winnowed the ranks. But it was good preparation for other, still more difficult tasks. I was determined to give this new challenge my utmost effort, and if that wasn't good enough, I would at least have the satisfaction of knowing I had tried. Small satisfaction, but some.

I had almost no idea what to expect on the morning of September 13, 1978, when I loaded my pickup, kissed my family goodbye, and set out on the five-hour drive up I-95 from Hunter Army Airfield in Savannah, Georgia, for Fort Bragg, North Carolina—and a challenge that would change my life forever.

CHAPTER**TWO**

Some army posts have a real beauty about them. The Presidio of Monterey, California, and the main post areas of Forts McClellan in Alabama and Benning in Georgia are a few that come to mind, principally because of the Spanish colonial architecture of the old buildings. Fort Stewart has magnificent live oaks and cypresses draped in Spanish moss.

But Fort Bragg, North Carolina, is about as drab and unappealing a spot as you can find in North America. The post sprawls over the Sandhills of North Carolina. It was established on near-worthless land as an artillery-training center during World War I. The land is sparsely covered with straggly pines and stunted scrub oak trees. The layout of the cantonment areas, the places where people live, seems haphazard. The whole place has an I'm-not-gonna-be-here-long feel about it.

But it is the "Home of the Airborne" and, as such, contains the Eighty-second Airborne Division, the Special Forces center and schools, the Fifth and Seventh Special Forces groups, the Eighteenth Airborne Corps headquarters, and the First Corps Support Command. There were also some smaller, miscellaneous organizations scattered in odd hidden corners around post. One of those was First Special Forces Operational Detachment–Delta.

I pulled into the parking lot of Moon Hall on the main post of Fort Bragg shortly before noon. I made my way into the lobby and saw a sign directing me to 1ST SFOD-D. I followed the arrow to the left and saw a man wearing unmarked fatigues sitting at a desk in a small room.

"Here for Selection, Sarge?" he asked.

"Yes, I am."

"Well, find your name and sign in here," he said as he indicated a roster on the desk and handed me a pen.

I eyed him on the sly while I found my name and wrote my signature next to it. He was about forty years old, soft-spoken, and good-looking. He wasn't exactly the type I had expected to meet. The first person I usually encountered when signing in to a new unit was some foul-tempered clerk. This man was not that at all.

"You won't be staying here; you'll be going to Aberdeen Camp. Have you ever been there before?" he asked as he looked me directly in the eyes.

When I told him that I had not, he handed me a strip map and explained how to find the place. It was on the western edge of post, about thirty miles away.

"Do you have a POV [privately owned vehicle] or do you need transportation?"

"No, I have my own vehicle."

He detached one sheet from the ream of orders I had given him.

"OK, Ranger. When you arrive at Aberdeen, park out front and report to the man at the gate. He'll square you away." As he handed me the rest of the orders, he said with a slight smile in his voice and on his face, "You have a good one, and I hope to see you later."

"Thanks," I replied. "I hope so too."

I took my time driving out to the camp. Aberdeen was what I had expected it to be—an isolation camp. These are small out-of-the-way places a unit can stay while planning for a deployment or a mission—secure spots offering refuge from the normal distractions of life. They have rustic barracks, a mess hall and offices for staff sections, a supply building and warehousing, a small motor pool, a landing zone for a few helicopters, and maybe a range for zeroing and test-firing weapons.

I was waved through the gate, and I parked in the lot nearby. The guy at the gate walked over as I was getting out of my truck. He was in fatigues without a name tag or insignia of any kind—unusual in the army. He stuck out his hand as we approached each other.

"Hello, Sergeant Haney, glad to have you here. Take your gear down to Barracks A and grab a bunk. Then find Sergeant Major Shumate. He'll get your equipment issued to you. Chow is at 1730[1]. Instructions for tomorrow will be posted on the board outside the mess hall. See you later. Have a good one."

"OK, thanks," I replied as I grabbed my kit bag and rucksack and headed in the direction of the barracks.

---

[1] The military uses the twenty-four-hour clock, a way of timekeeping in which the day runs from midnight to midnight and is divided into twenty-four hours. As with everything the military does, there's precise logic behind it. For instance, there's no possibility of confusing seven in the morning (0700) with seven at night (1900).

The barracks were the standard "tropical hooches,"[2] low-frame buildings twenty-four feet wide and seventy-two feet long. Concrete floors and tin roofs with wide overhanging eaves. The upper halves of the walls were hinged on top and propped open at a forty-five-degree angle to serve as windows. The open "windows" were screened. A row of GI cots ran down each side of the building, and a string of bare lightbulbs hung from the centerline of the exposed rafters. Not a bad home at all.

I went about halfway down the building, found a bunk on the left side, and dropped my bags. My idea was to get away from the door and avoid as much traffic and stirred-up dust as I could.

There were eight or ten other men in the hooch. Their shoulder patches showed them to be from overseas units and from some of the forts out west. I nodded to the ones who looked up as I went out to find the sergeant major.

I stepped out the door and took a look around. There was a warehouse-looking building near the motor pool. Probably a good place to start. About halfway there I met a guy hurrying up the sidewalk.

"Hey, bud, do you know where I can find Sergeant Major Shumate?" I asked.

"Yeah, that's him over by the deuce-and-a-half." He pointed at a man standing next to an army two-and-a-half-ton truck.

"OK, if you say so." I started over to see this alleged sergeant major.

---

[2] Temporary shelters. In the field, hooches can be built out of anything that happens to be available, including snow.

Sergeant majors are the walking, breathing embodiment of Everything That's Right in the U.S. Army: hard-as-nails soldiers with the pride of a lion and creases in their uniforms sharp enough to cut meat. This guy looked like a bum. His shirt was wide open, showing his belly, and he wore no T-shirt. His dog tags were gold plated. His hat was tipped up on the back of his head, and he wore a huge elaborately curled and waxed handlebar mustache.

There was trickery of some kind here. The only thing I expected on this trip was the unexpected. So, if this was a game, I figured I'd play along and see what happened.

I stepped three paces in front of the man, slammed to a halt, and from the rigid position of parade rest[3] barked, "Sergeant Major, I was told to see you and draw some equipment!"

He eyed me for a second or so as the wrinkles of a grin crawled from beneath his mustache to settle around his eyes.

"Dang, Ranger, relax a little bit, will you? This ain't no promotion board. You keep that up, you're gonna wear me out." His voice was rumbling and rich, with a tinge of the hills deep within.

It was force of habit. In the Rangers, when we addressed a senior NCO (noncommissioned officer), we stood at parade rest. I relaxed slightly to the position of at ease.[4]

"That's a little better," he said. His grin widened. He didn't seem to be making fun of me; he just appeared surprised at being addressed in such a formal manner.

[3] Parade rest is commanded only from the position of attention. Feet are parallel, ten inches apart. Eyes rigidly straight ahead, hands centered behind the back at belt level, right hand on top. There's nothing restful about it.
[4] Same as parade rest except you can move your head to look at whomever is talking to you.

"Go over to the supply shack, get yourself a bag of equipment, and sign your name on the roster at the door. Don't worry about getting it too clean when you turn it in. Everybody knows my standards ain't very high."

Man. This was shaping up to be a strange place. I hustled down to the supply shack, signed for a bag of equipment, and talked to the guy on duty while I checked the contents of the bag against the equipment list.

"Is that guy up there really a sergeant major?"

"Shumate? Yeah, he really is. He's the sergeant major in charge of Selection."

"Well, he's certainly different from any sergeant major I've ever met before."

"He's different from any *human being* you've ever met before."

Sergeant Major Walter J. Shumate was a living legend in Special Forces. A veteran who had entered the army during the Korean War, he had seen and done it all. Now closing in on thirty years of service, at forty-four he was the oldest man ever to make it through Delta Force Selection. And he was invaluable to the formation of the unit. Shumate added an element of humanity that could very well have eluded the organization in those critical early years. Without his special touch and unique influence, the outfit could easily have taken itself way too seriously. But with Shumate around, no matter how special we thought we were, he could always convince us that we were just human beings. He was serious about soldiering, but he was the opposite of a robot.

Barracks A was starting to fill up when I returned. So far, everyone was from somewhere other than Fort Bragg. There were a few guys I knew from various courses we had attended together, and two I had served with in other units. As large as the army was in those days, I had been around long enough that I knew someone no matter where I went. A few guys were loudly expounding their expertise on special operations and counterterrorism (CT) as I walked down the aisle to my bunk.

Trying to impress each other with a lot of talk, I thought. First Ranger Battalion had been working for almost a year with the army's interim CT force, Blue Light, trying to develop techniques for combating terrorist action. Both units had worked pretty hard at it, but after a couple of joint exercises and thorough after-action analysis, it was apparent we weren't making much headway. In fact, the last exercise had gone so badly that our battalion commander had been relieved of command. So far, no one was very experienced with, much less expert at, what it would take to engage and defeat terrorism.

A guy was sitting on the bunk next to mine, unpacking his kit bag. He looked up as I put my equipment down. Our eyes met and we both put out a hand.

"Keekee Saenz, Three/Seven Special Forces—Panama," he told me with a slight Hispanic accent.

We shook hands. "Eric Haney, First Ranger. *Mucho gusto en conocerlo*, Keekee," I replied.

"*El gusto es mío*," he returned with a smile.

Keekee was a medium-sized guy, with the wiry muscled build of a runner. His hair was thick but short, and he wore a pencil-thin mustache. He looked about my age, twenty-six or so. He had the air of a tough, competent soldier.

"Keekee, y'all heard much about this outfit down in Panama?" I asked as I sorted my equipment.

24

"Probably not much more than you have," he said. "Everything about this group has been very close-hold.[5] One of our guys made it here in the spring, but no one's heard anything from him since."

"We had one try out too, last spring," I said. "But he was back after the first week and he won't say a word. So far information has been pretty tight. I guess we'll find out what we need to know as we go along."

"*Ojalá*," he said, turning back to his gear.

"*Sí, ojalá.*" *Yes, God willing indeed.*

I finished unpacking, then changed into running shoes and shorts and went out for a run. The afternoon was too beautiful to waste sitting around the barracks. As I went out the gate, the guy on duty nodded and said, "Have a good 'un."

"Have a good one" must be the unit mantra, I thought as I jogged away from the camp. The atmosphere of this place was so relaxed, I felt slightly uneasy. All could not be what it seemed.

As I ran along and worked up a good sweat, I tried to imagine what this "selection course" would be like. But I had no frame of reference to make a determination from. This was unlike anything I had seen in the army. So far, it was just a bunch of guys gathering at an out-of-the-way camp administered by what looked like a bunch of military hobos. I would just keep my mouth shut, keep my eyes and ears open, and respond to whatever came up. It was the system I'd always used in new situations, and so far it had served me well.

Lost in the privacy of my thoughts, I ran for miles over

[5] Close-hold: secret.

the pine-clad hills, listening to the rhythm of my feet on the ground. Happily soaked in sweat, I made my way back to camp, where I waved to the guy at the gate, who replied with a nod and a smile. I headed for the showers, took my time cleaning up, and went to supper.

The mess hall was full and noisy. I sat at a table with several guys from units in Germany. We had a few friends in common. They said about fifty guys had come over from Europe to attend Selection. Looked like there was going to be quite a crowd.

Chow was remarkably good for a field camp. I finished, turned in my tray and utensils, and went outside to read the bulletin board. It said:

> 14 September 1978
> Formation: 0600 hrs.
> Uniform: Boots, fatigues, soft caps
>   (no berets)
> ID Cards and Dog Tags

The message was clear enough. No overload of information there. But some people would be annoyed by the "no berets" part. Berets were badges of honor then, limited to elite troops who had earned them.

I heard someone from the 101st Airborne Division ask a cadre[6] member if we were restricted to camp. He was told there was no restriction; just take the information from the bulletin board, no more and no less.

---

[6] The permanent members of a temporary unit. A student in high school, for example, is temporarily a senior. But the faculty are the cadre, the permanent members, of the school.

A lot of guys won't be able to handle that, I thought. *They'll be in the NCO Club tonight and hung over in the morning. Should be interesting.*

I lounged around outside for a while and talked with a few acquaintances. Then I returned to the barracks, finished arranging and putting away my gear, and read for a while.

At 2030 I rolled up in my poncho liner[7] and enjoyed the feeling of stretching out on a bunk. Not bad at all. As a Ranger, I was more accustomed to sleeping on the ground than in a bed. This was nearly luxurious. I rolled onto my side, pulled a corner of the poncho liner over my head, and went to sleep.

Seasoned soldiers have the ability to fall asleep almost immediately. Like food and water, sleep is a commodity we take whenever we can get it. I wasn't buying this laid-back routine at all. If this was like Ranger School, someone would come screaming into the barracks after midnight, to destroy our rest and play mind games. Barring any middle-of-the-night disturbances, I would wake myself at 0515.

I woke promptly at 0512 and lay there for a few minutes, listening to the sound of the sleeping barracks.

The extra sleep that morning felt good. Back at battalion,[8] I was always up at 0430 and in the barracks by 0500 for a cup of coffee with my squad leaders before they got the troops up at 0530.

I slid out of the bunk, put on shorts and shower shoes, grabbed my shaving kit, and went to the latrine to get squared

[7] A blanketlike tie-in liner for a rain poncho. It's made of a lightweight but strong material that holds in body heat. It's about the most versatile tool a soldier has. You can find one at most army-navy surplus stores.
[8] Battalion: headquarters.

away. The air was chill and crisp. There was no moon, and the stars were still bright. I like this "in-between" time of day. The world is silent and still, the night creatures are back in their hideaways, and the day animals aren't stirring yet.

When I came out of the latrine, other men were up and moving about, and vehicle lights were coming through the gate. Half of the guys in the barracks were still in their bunks as I dressed and laced on my jungle boots. They were my oldest pair of field boots, which had been oiled with neat's-foot until they were as soft as moccasins. A soldier doesn't need much in the way of uniforms, but good boots are indispensable. I made sure I had a notebook and pen in my breast pocket and then went outside.

The parking lot was rapidly filling up, and a number of guys were ambling to the center of the compound. Glowing cigarette tips illuminated faces, and quiet voices drifted about the area.

"Haney! What the hell you doin' here?" a voice brayed at me from the darkness.

There was only one person with a voice like that. I turned and said, "Hello, Parks. How did you ever find your way here?"

Virgil Parks was a bona fide, twenty-four-karat, dyed-in-the-wool character. Virg had joined the U.S. Army in 1968 specifically to go to Vietnam, and he had been a Ranger ever since. We had been platoon sergeants in the same company until the year before, when he transferred to Fort Benning to be an instructor at Ranger School.

I could only imagine he was here because he had worn out his welcome with the Ranger Department. He had a habit of doing that wherever he went. He was eccentric to the point of lunacy—and that takes some doing in the Ranger world. Parks went full blast and unaimed at all times. He was utterly unable to modulate his output of energy to the task at hand.

He closed his eyes, tilted his impressive nose up in that peculiar fashion of his, and took a long drag off the cigarette he held between his thumb and forefinger. "Just thought I'd come and see what these yahoos are up to around here. 'Sides, the Ranger Department's turning into a bunch of sissies. They're even going to issue a candy bar every day to the little troopies in Florida Phase during the winter classes, just 'cause those sissies froze to death last year."

There was nothing "sissy" about that tragedy. During the Florida Phase of Ranger School, students received only one C ration[9] a day. They were expending calories at a much higher rate than they were taking them in at and were already in a weakened state from the previous phases of the course. If the temperature of the swamp water they were constantly in fell too low, they were in real danger of hypothermia.

It had happened during a particularly cold night on a patrol the previous winter. Twenty-three men had gone into hypothermia on a night crossing of the Yellow River. Four died in the swamps. The Ranger cadre had crossed that fine line between hardhead and bonehead, and men had died as a result. I was surprised no one had been court-martialed[10] over that affair.

---

[9] Canned field ration. Nowadays, soldiers eat MREs—meals ready to eat.

[10] Court-martial: a military court set up to punish members of the army, air force, navy, and marines for serious offenses. The Uniform Code of Military Justice is similar to, but not the same as, the American legal code.

"Yeah, I've heard that." There was no use reasoning with Parks; he was impervious to logic.

A line of deuce-and-a-halves pulled up and parked while we were talking. At two minutes until six, a guy with a clipboard in his hand walked out of the HQ shack. He was dressed in jeans, a T-shirt, and a baseball cap. He stood at the edge of the crowd and looked at us dispassionately until everyone became quiet.

"Fall in, in four ranks," he called. We shuffled into formation in about a minute. The 163 men gathered there stood at attention.

"At ease! Listen up! Sound off when I call your name, and get on the truck I've indicated. If your name's not called, stand fast and I'll get to you. Truck number one . . ." He started calling names in alphabetical order.

Each truck had a big chalk numeral on its tailgate. When my name was called, I shouted "Here!" and climbed aboard. Soon the trucks got under way, and we rumbled out the gate just as the sun splashed its rays over the eastern horizon.

Fifteen minutes later, we halted along the edge of what looked like a drop zone. "Holland DZ" I heard some of the Fort Bragg troops say as we dismounted.

Sergeant Major Shumate was standing nearby wearing khaki pants, a Hawaiian shirt, and a Panama hat. "Fall in on me, ladies!" he called. "Make it six ranks. I want a tight formation."

As we were forming up, somebody approached with a camera and tripod and prepared to take a photograph of the formation.

"What's this about, Walt?" an anonymous voice squawked from somewhere in the crowd.

"This is going to be the 'before' picture of this group, my young darlings, and we'll take a second shot in a few weeks," Shumate replied.

I was aghast that someone had called a sergeant major by his first name, yet Shumate seemed to take no offense. But when a small cluster of the men started laughing and yahooing from within the group, as if this was some sort of stupid joke, Shumate became steely. The friendliness in his voice came to a screeching halt, and he growled in a volcanic tone, "Yeah, well, we'll see who's laughing when you dirtbags are finished and the next picture I take is about half the size of this front rank standing here. The serious ones will be in that photo, and the rest of you will be back home, lying to your teammates about why you didn't make it. So since you loudmouths—and a bunch more of you besides—won't be here for the 'after' photo, I'll just have my laugh at you boneheads right now—har-de-har-har!"

It was a sober group he addressed now as he called us to attention. The photographer took the shot and departed.

Shumate continued as though nothing had happened. "This is the Ranger/Special Forces physical training test. Your graders for events one through four are arranged behind me, from left to right. When I call your name, go to the grader indicated. Have a good one. Event number one!" He started calling off names. I fell in on my grader.

The army had four PT tests in those days. There were a test for staff and support troops, a more strenuous test for the combat arms, a test for jump school, and the Ranger/Special Forces test. Today's tests are similar, but not exactly the same. And they're critical. When physical fitness can make the difference between life and death, it's important to take it pretty seriously.

The first three tests had a descending grade scale based on age. The older a person was, the less he had to perform for a given score. For the Ranger/SF test, age received no breaks; everyone was graded at the seventeen-year-old level. The test consisted of push-ups, sit-ups, the run-dodge-jump, the inverted crawl (known as the perverted crawl), and the two-mile run. The uniform for the test was fatigues and combat boots; running shoes were not yet in style in the army. Shirts could be removed in warm weather. My first event was the run-dodge-jump. This was an agility and quickness drill. It consisted of taking off from the starting line, sprinting forward to a set of gates perpendicular to the path, running through them and then jumping a ditch, sprinting to a second set of gates, going through those, then around and back through them again, over the ditch, back through the first set of gates, repeating the whole process once more, and finishing at the starting point. I usually completed this event in about thirteen seconds. A time of fifteen seconds earned a score of one hundred. Minimum passing time was nineteen seconds.

I ran through the event in my normal time. A grader handed me my scorecard and directed me to the push-up station. I fell into line and had barely recovered my breath when I was called forward and told to assume the starting position.

I had just gotten into position and asked my grader to count out loud for me when the "go" command was given. When the grader had counted to fifty-three, I stopped and rested on my hands and knees with a few seconds to spare. I had found that the easiest way to get through this test was to breathe like a runaway steam engine and do the push-ups as fast as possible. I just had to make sure I did them all correctly, or the grader would not count them.

Time was called. I was given my card and sent to the inverted crawl—an event that ranks as one of the stupidest things ever imagined. Whereas other events on the PT test measured things such as agility or upper body strength, the inverted crawl measured . . . well, no one had the faintest idea what it measured.

On the command "go," you lifted your butt off the ground and crawled, crablike, with your back to the ground and torso facing skyward. In this position you "sprinted" forward, feet first, for twenty meters, then straight back, hands first, unable to see where you were going, all the way back to the starting point.

I executed the event, received a max score, picked the sandspurs from my hands, and went to the sit-up station. It was obvious to me now that there was no rest between events. As soon as I finished one station, I went directly to another without waiting around. Everything was organized and businesslike. There was no shouting or any other form of normal military dramatics—and there was no way to slip to the back of a line and catch any rest between events.

I was motioned forward for the sit-ups. On my back, fingers interlaced behind my head, knees bent, and the grader holding my feet. The cool sand felt good on my back as I waited for the command to start. Then the command "go." I was knocking them out as fast as I could while in my peripheral vision I could see other bodies slamming up and down. *We look like pistons in an engine,* I thought as I finished the exercise and fell back on the ground to take a breath before getting to my feet and retrieving my scorecard.

A minute or two later, all the events were finished and we were called over to the trucks for a loose formation.

"Make sure your fatigue jackets are on the truck you arrived in," announced Shumate. "Then fall in on the grader you had for your last event." He motioned to the graders standing on the dirt road to our right.

"Okay. Do it," he barked.

I folded my shirt and put it under the bench of my truck, then made my way down to my grader for the start of the two-mile run. The grader took our scorecards and gave each of us a red cloth bib to hang around our neck. As he gave us the bibs, he also assigned each of us a different number. My number was six. The other groups had other colors.

Then Shumate called us to the start line.

"Okay, ladies, we've all done this once or twice before in our lives. On the command 'go,' take off. Stay on this road for two miles to the finish point. As you come into the finish, look for your grader; he will be holding up a panel with the same color you're wearing. Everyone ready . . . *Go!*"

And off we went. At first it was the same cluster as in the start of any race. Some guys sprinted off; others hung back and let the crowd thin a bit. I took the middle course. I'm a good runner but not a great one. Within a couple hundred meters, I was able to settle into my pace and hold the speed I liked. Soon I stretched my stride a little and galloped down the road. This beat the heck out of running around a track, the usual setting for a PT test. Sooner than I had expected, I could see the finish point. The gazelles were already crossing the line.

I stretched out my stride a little more and concentrated on blowing the spent air from my lungs in order to breathe more deeply. I was running beside someone and we were matched pace for pace. As I tried to pull ahead, he stayed with me. I glanced over at the man. It was Keekee Saenz. Soon we were running flat out, with neither of us able to outpace the other.

I saw my grader up ahead and then heard the timekeeper calling out the minutes and seconds. "Twelve minutes, fifty seconds—fifty-one, fifty-two, fifty-three, fifty-four," he shouted as I crossed the finish line, made eye contact, and yelled, "Red six!" to my grader.

"Roger, red six," he replied as he marked down the time.

I slowed my pace to a trot and continued down the road for a hundred meters or so before coming to a walk. I put my hands on my hips and walked back to the finish point as my breathing returned to normal. When I got near the finish line, one of the cadre members told me to go down the road to where the trucks were now parked, retrieve my shirt, and stand by for instructions. Back down the road I went.

The trucks must have gone around us by another route, because there they were, lined up in order, about three hundred meters down the dirt track.

As I neared them, I saw Sergeant Major Shumate talking to someone. He looked up as I got my fatigue shirt from the truck.

"Having fun, Ranger?" he asked as I buttoned it up.

"I sure am, Sergeant Major. Where to next?"

He eyed me from under lowered brows. "You look a little heated. Why don't you go down to the lake and have yourself a dip? Someone down there will give you instructions. And"—he paused deliberately, so I stopped to look at him—"have a good 'un."

I walked to the edge of the lake, where a small group was gathering. A short, sandy-haired guy motioned for me to join them.

"This is the swim test, men. From the buoys on this side to the buoys on the other side is one hundred meters. Uniform for the swim is combat boots and fatigues. This is not a timed exercise. You may use any stroke you desire, but you may not stop until you have reached the buoys on the other side. Wade out to the first set of buoys and start swimming. Don't put your feet down until you have reached the other set of buoys. At that time, you will be instructed to stand up and wade out. No questions? Okay, have a good 'un."

The dozen or so of us in the group waded out into the water. It was coffee-colored and as warm as a bath. The water was at the middle of my chest when I reached the line of buoys. I sank down to my neck to let the air out of my clothes, then started to swim. First I did a sidestroke on my left side and then rolled over to my right. About two-thirds of the way across, I rolled onto my back and backstroked the rest of the way. If there is any secret to swimming while clothed, it is that you have to relax and not hurry. You're still buoyant; you just have more drag to contend with.

The swim wasn't bad at all. For the Ranger swim test, we were blindfolded and walked off a high dive, fully dressed and armed, carrying an M16. After hitting the water, we swam to the side of the pool and climbed out. The point of the test was to simulate walking off a stream bank at night. If we could successfully complete the test, we weren't likely to panic if we suddenly and unexpectedly found ourselves in deep water and unable to see. I was sure this test was just to see if we were confident and comfortable in the water.

I climbed out of the lake and moved up the bank to a stand of large pine trees. Then I took my uniform off, wrung the water out, and re-dressed. I didn't have to empty my jungle boots because they drained themselves. Drying my hair wasn't a problem either. I was wearing the Ranger standard "high and tight"—about a quarter inch of hair on top and white sidewalls.

I walked down to a cadre member who was watching the people still in the water. Men were in the lake from one side to the other now, some crawling out and others getting in. A safety boat flanked each side and moved back and forth as the lifeguards aboard kept an eye on the weaker swimmers. I saw one guy on the other side of the lake walk out to his waist, shake his head, and then walk back to shore. I guessed he knew his limitations.

About halfway across the lake, one of the boats moved to a man floundering at the edge of the pack. The lifeguards waited nearby until it looked as if he was in serious trouble, then extended a pole to him. He grabbed it in desperation and was pulled to the side of the boat, where he clung like a tick on a dog's ear. Another one down.

A small group of us had now made it across the lake, and a steady trickle of men was coming up the bank. The cadre member pointed to a truck and told us to mount up for the ride back to camp when we had a full load. We were to follow the new instructions posted on the bulletin board.

We arrived back at camp and checked the board.

Lunch: C ration
Supper: 1700
Formation: 1830
Uniform: Fatigues with soft cap, rucksack weighing 40 lbs., two canteens of water

A set of scales hung from the chin-up bar in front of the mess hall. A stack of C ration cases stood next to the bulletin board. I fished out two (one for lunch, one to stash—just in case) and went to the hooch to change into a dry uniform. It was still only 1030, so there was a lot of time to kill.

I changed into dry clothes, then walked around camp just to pass the time. There was a long line of men at the orderly room, out-processing. They were the ones who had failed the PT test or the swim test. I wondered what the heck they had even come here for if they couldn't pass a simple PT test. Some of the guys had come over from units in Europe—which was a pretty expensive trip just to flunk out within the first few hours.

I overheard a couple of guys from SF grousing that it wasn't fair and saying they should be allowed a retest. I recognized one of the men in the "Go Home" line as a sergeant first class I knew from the Twenty-fifth Division in Hawaii. We nodded to each other in mutual recognition, but he didn't look as if he wanted to talk.

CHAPTER**THREE**

My rucksack registered forty-two pounds when I hung it on the scales just before supper. I took it back to the hooch and added what seemed to be about three pounds, then fastened two canteens of water to the lower sides of it. I wanted to be able to get at them without taking my rucksack off. And I wanted my load to weigh a bit more than prescribed, just in case the scales were a little off.

Normally I would also be wearing my load bearing equipment (LBE). This consists of a pistol belt and its shoulder harness, to which are attached magazine and first-aid pouches, compass, strobe light, knife or bayonet, canteens, and other odds and ends. The LBE is our fighting load; it is how we carry our ammunition and the items we need to fight and survive in combat. Loaded for combat, it weighs about forty pounds. The rucksack is then worn over the top of the LBE. The bulletin board instructions, however, said nothing about LBE, and I intended to follow instructions to the letter.

At 1830 we boarded trucks for a trip across Fort Bragg. Some of the local guys said we were on Chicken Road, a wide sandy tank trail leading straight as an arrow through the sparse pines and scrub oaks of the monotonous Sandhills. I'd never seen an uglier place. We bumped and swayed along, shrouded within a fog bank of gritty truck-churned dust.

After about thirty minutes, we came to a stop at a crossroads, where we dismounted. Sergeant Major Shumate stood nearby, watching us with a challenging grin.

"All right, y'all, gather round; we don't need a formation—a cluster will do," he said as we grabbed our rucksacks and formed a semicircle around him.

"Well, our happy little band is slightly smaller than it was this morning, isn't it?" Shumate asked. "What, no comments? Then let us proceed. This event is the eighteen-mile rucksack march. In case this is a mystery to you, we call it that because from here to the finish point is eighteen miles, and you will be carrying a rucksack while you march.

"Complete the march as fast as you can. Stay on this road. Don't accept rides from strangers. Don't give piggyback rides to one another. Cadre members will be posted along the way. They will be holding green chem lights. As you go past, give them your color and number. The finish point is where this road hits the pavement of King Road. A cadre member will be there to mark your finish time. Water is available along the route. You may quit at any time; to do so, merely give your color and number to any cadre member and tell him, 'I voluntarily withdraw.' He will ask you no questions. If you wish to withdraw now, just stand fast when the others depart."

No one moved or spoke.

"Since there are no questions"—he looked at his watch—

"time will start in two minutes. Direction of march is north." He pointed in the direction from which we had come.

"I won't fire a gun or anything. Put your rucks on and depart when I call go. And . . . have a good 'un." I mumbled the last part along with him under my breath.

Eighteen miles. I wondered how they had come up with that distance. It seemed a little odd. The Ranger battalion standard for a twenty-miler was six hours, and that was with weapon, full combat equipment, and steel pot (helmet) locked on the head. I was much lighter than that, and this would be a night march on a cool, dry evening. I would try for four and a half hours. That would equal four miles an hour, or a mile every fifteen minutes. *No, that's too fast. I can't do that without running, and I'm not gonna run. Five hours would be a good time.* I was certain that no one in the army had a faster standard for road marching than the Rangers.

Shumate called go, and off we went. A dozen or so guys took off running, most of them in pairs. Another group of perhaps thirty men tore off at a furious walking pace. *To each his own,* I thought, and concentrated on settling into my stride and getting my rucksack situated on my back. Within a few minutes, the crowd at the starting point had spread out and I had room to establish my pace.

Eighteen miles is a long way, and it can't be done at a sprint. That had been the distance of the graduation swim when I had attended the Special Forces/Scout Swimmer course in Greece in 1972. I suddenly remembered something: Country Grimes, the man who recruited me for Selection, had been my senior instructor for that course.

After about two miles I was warmed up and moving well.

41

I like to walk. Breathing in sync with the movement of arms and legs, shirt and fly unbuttoned to let the air circulate—it all feels good. On a long, hard march, my mind slips off to a place of its own and my body switches to autopilot. It makes for a private, interior time in an otherwise highly socialized military existence. It's also when I hatch some of my better plots and schemes.

Within four miles I was catching up with and passing some of the runners. I planned to march for two hours before taking a breather and then take a few minutes' break every hour. It was full dark now, but the ambient light was pretty good and the white sand of the road showed all the holes and furrows to be avoided. All in all, a pretty good route.

When I was about seven miles into the march, I saw a cluster of lights up ahead on the side of the road, with shadowy figures moving among them. As I got closer, I saw several trucks circled around a group of trees with their lights illuminating some kind of activity.

As I approached, a cadre member beckoned me over. I gave him my color and number, and he told me to drop my rucksack under any one of a set of scales dangling from a pole tied between two trees and fill my canteens from the water cans on the back of one of the trucks. I dropped my rucksack, grabbed my canteens, and drained one straight down as I walked over to find the water cans. Without my rucksack I felt light enough to fly. But that would change in a few more hours. I watched the activity in the circle of light as I took another drink and filled my canteens.

When I walked back over to the scales, I saw an interesting

exchange between one of the walkers and a man who seemed to be the cadre member in charge of the site.

The cadre was saying, "Sarge, your rucksack is light. It doesn't meet the forty-pound requirement."

Before he could continue, the walker interrupted, saying, "Well, it's got to be close. How much *does* it weigh?"

"I really can't tell you," the cadre replied in a monotone. "If you look at the scales, you'll see they don't register anything less than forty pounds. So as far as we're concerned, your rucksack weighs nothing."

I looked up at the set of scales above my rucksack and saw that he was correct. The face was painted a solid white until it reached the forty-pound mark.

The cadre continued. "And since you're carrying nothing, the only way you can meet the weight requirement is to take this." He reached behind him and handed the guy a big ragged piece of concrete that looked as if it had come from a roadbed that had been dug up. "I weighed this myself," he went on, "and certify it as weighing exactly forty pounds. Now, for you to continue the march, you will sign for this item, strap it to your rucksack, and turn it in at the finish point when you complete the march. Any questions?"

The walker stood there holding the chunk of concrete against his chest while a half-smirking, half-incredulous look materialized on his face. I recognized him as one of the loudmouths who had been ready with a comment all day, but he was quiet now.

He looked up at the cadre in front of him and asked in a pleading voice, "Marvin, are you serious?"

So they knew each other. This was getting better.

"Completely" was the reply.

The guy thought for a few more seconds and then said, "No, I can't do that." He dropped the concrete and stood with his arms hanging down by his sides.

"Are you voluntarily withdrawing from the course?"

A pause. "Yes, I guess I am."

"Take your ruck and get on the back of that truck." The cadre chief indicated a vehicle off to the side of the rest.

The guy stood there a beat or two longer, looking as if he couldn't believe what had happened. Our eyes met, and he gave a slight shrug of acceptance, then picked up his rucksack and moved away. That little exchange sure got my attention—and the attention of everyone else who witnessed it.

I grabbed my rucksack and asked the cadre who had weighed it, "Good to go?" as I put my arms through the straps.

"Yep, you can roll," he said as he scribbled something on a clipboard. Then he looked up and said to me as I got the rucksack settled on my back, "Have a good 'un."

I was out of the circle of light and back onto the road in a few steps. I was glad to be away from there. That had been some scene. The cadre chief had never been loud or threatening, and he had never spoken in a demeaning or insulting manner, but it had been clear he would neither listen to nor tolerate any bullshit. I liked that style. The seriousness of this was starting to feel genuine.

The rest of the march was . . . well, just a night rucksack march. After twelve miles I was tired, my feet hurt, my shoulders ached, and I was soaked in sweat.

I hit the finish point on King Road at a few minutes

under five hours of march time. The cadre member logged me in on his clipboard and told me it was only two miles back to camp, there was soup in the mess hall, new instructions were on the bulletin board, and have a good 'un.

I took my time on the walk back to camp. I dropped my ruck by my cot and went to the mess hall for a canteen cup of soup. There were about a dozen other footsore and tired guys in the mess hall, but every one of them wore a look of contentment. It came from completing a strenuous task and knowing they'd done well. Completing a road march is no huge triumph, but it's one of those many small things in life by which we measure ourselves.

Also, the soup was pretty darn good. One of the things the army always does right is soup. It's prepackaged, and the cooks make it in fifteen-gallon pots, but you can always count on it to be steaming hot, and it's just the ticket when you're footsore and tired and the sweat you're soaked in is starting to chill. It's a simple thing, but it makes a difference.

I said good night to the guys in the mess hall and headed for the shower. A little after 0100 hours, I checked the bulletin board. It said:

1000 hours
Classroom

I hit my cot, wrapped up in my poncho liner, and slept the sleep of the righteous.

1000 hours. Sore feet; stiff leg, back, and shoulder muscles. Seated in the classroom. A closed folder and a couple of sharp pencils on the desk in front of me, and a smiling guy up front giving instructions.

"Just a questionnaire about yourselves, men," he said, smiling. "It's not timed. Answer every question and give each question your best answer. If something is unclear or confusing, give it your best guess. If something completely stumps you, I'll be at the back of the room. This is strictly an individual effort, no collaboration. Okay, open your booklets and begin."

I opened the cover: a psychological test. And it would be the first of many. Throughout Selection we took these tests over and over again. Each was worded a bit differently than the others, with questions crafted a little differently, but the tests and the questions were essentially the same. We always took the tests when we were tired—but not when we were exhausted.

By answering the same questions over and over, at seemingly random times, an individual was less likely to be able to sustain duplicity or deception. The same held true for being testing while fatigued. The person who may be trying to craft a lie has less energy to put into the effort. It becomes easier to tell the truth when you can't remember what you might have said last time.

But this was the first test of its kind that I had ever taken. Most of the questions seemed to have an obvious point: Do you hear voices? Are you an agent of God? Are people following you? Are you often misunderstood? Do you have thoughts too terrible to speak about?

The only ones I really wondered about were the several variations of "Is your stool black and tarry?" That question was in every exam throughout Selection. Years later, during the annual mental evaluation of the unit, I asked the psychologist about that question and why it had been asked so often. The answer was straightforward and made a lot of sense.

"Oh," he said, "black and tarry stool is an indication of blood in the digestive system, which could mean ulcers or indicate someone with a drinking problem."

Very sensible.

An hour later I finished the questionnaire, closed the folder, and carried the material to the cadre member at the back of the room. "Smiley" cautioned me not to speak about the test and told me that new instructions were on the bulletin board.

I stepped outside and blinked in the bright sunshine. The camp was quiet. A line of men was outside the orderly room for out-processing. Some looked a little sheepish, and some covered up their embarrassment with bluster or nonchalance.

I checked the bulletin board and saw that there was nothing scheduled until PT formation the next morning. The rest of the day and night was free.

I went to Barracks B to see about a comrade. Joe McAdams was an old-timer from our Ranger company who had gone into Special Forces the previous year. I had not seen him, but I'd heard he was in the Selection course. That morning at chow, Parks had told me that Joe had been injured on the previous night's march and was in his cot, waiting for his unit to send someone to pick him up.

Must have turned an ankle, I thought as I walked into the hooch and scanned the line of bunks for Mac.

"Hey, Haney. Down here," he called, and gave a languid wave from a cot midway down the building.

"Lord almighty, Mac, what happened to you?" I asked as

47

I got close enough to see the raw, bloody soles of his propped-up feet.

"Pads of my feet stayed in my boots when I took 'em off after the road march."

From toe to heel, the bottoms of his feet were completely devoid of skin. It looked as though some ancient Indian warrior had scalped his feet instead of his head. That raw, naked flesh must have hurt like hell exposed to the air.

"Yeah, it smarts a mite," he said, reading my mind. "You know what happened? All those old Ranger calluses were still on my feet, but they weren't very well anchored anymore. I haven't done any rucksack marching since I got out of phase training [Special Forces qualification training] a year ago. The medic said that during the march last night, I got blisters under the old calluses and eventually the whole mess just came loose. Now, ain't that something?"

"Yeah, Mac. It is," I said, wincing at the sight of his feet. "Looks like you'll be on your back for a while."

"Reckon so," he replied, taking a drag from the cigarette he had just lit. "Guess I'll get a chance to catch up on my reading now."

"I guess you will. Are you squared away? Somebody coming to get you?"

"My team medic is coming out with an FLA [field litter ambulance] to pick me up, and the group surgeon is going to meet us at Womack Army Hospital. Probably spend a day at the hospital to clean 'em and treat for infection, and then go on convalescent leave until I can grow some new skin," he said, waggling his feet.

"You need anything?" I asked as I got up to leave.

"Nah, I'm OK. Medic'll be here soon and I got plenty of cigarettes, so I'll just take it easy until he gets here."

"OK, partner, you hang in there. And tell any of the old gang you see that I said hello."

"Will do, man. You do the same—and come and see me when you finish here."

"Sure, Mac. Take care."

We shook hands and I left, walking away with the image of those obscenely skinned feet in my mind. I was left wondering again where that line between hard and stupid was. But I guessed that was an individual determination. Mac had found it the night before, somewhere along those eighteen miles.

Joe McAdams immediately went into army legend as "The Guy Who Walked His Feet Off in Delta Force Selection." Everybody knew the myth, but few ever knew the man. Now you do.

The next morning, we fell in for PT at 0600. Because I hate running in the middle of a formation, I maneuvered a spot on the right end of the front rank that would put me in the front of the formation for the run. It's always best to be the lead dog. The scenery's better.

As we were getting into formation, before a cadre member came out to take charge, I heard more than the usual laughter from back in the group. I looked behind me to see what was going on, and there was a guy standing in formation wearing a gorilla mask that covered his entire head.

His rank insignia said he was a captain, his shoulder patch said he was in Special Forces, and the mask he wore said he was a nitwit. As the twittering died away, no-nonsense

Marvin stepped out of the orderly room to take charge of the formation.

"Group! Aaaten-*shun*!" he called. "Stand at . . . *ease*!

"Just some light PT to loosen up before we start the day, men. And since my voice is a little hoarse this morning, I'm gonna need some help calling cadence. Let's see." He scanned the group. "Yeah you, Gorilla Man. Get up here and call cadence for me."

Gorilla Man made a move to take off his mask.

"No," Marvin snapped. "Leave the mask on. You'll take it off when I tell you to. This is my formation and you'll follow my instructions."

We then extended ranks for PT, and Marvin put us through one helluva pace of calisthenics. Gorilla Man was shouting the cadence *and* exercising while Marvin shouted at him.

Side straddle hops, the high jumper, squat thrusts, push-ups, turn and bounce. We continued the furious pace until the Masked Moron finally went to his knees, hyperventilating inside his mask.

"Get back in the formation," Marvin told him. "Keep the mask. It suits you. Now, group! Aaaten—*shun*! Close ranks! *March*! Chow's on in the mess hall. Take your instructions from the bulletin board. Fall out!"

As the formation fell out with nervous laughter, I watched Gorilla Man pull the mask off his soaking wet head and blanched face. He walked away, looking confused by what had happened. I could not fathom what he had expected. Applause?

The bulletin board announced another formation at 0800. Plenty of time to clean up and have breakfast.

We fell in at 0800 and, from there, filed through the

warehouse, where we each picked up a machine-gun ammo canister. Once we were back in formation, the cadre member in charge had us open and inspect the contents of the emergency canisters we all now had.

I opened my can, took out the items it contained, and checked them off against the list that the cadre was reading out loud.

> URC-68 emergency signaling radio
> VS-17 aircraft signaling panel
> Signal mirror
> Red smoke grenade[1]
> Purple smoke grenade[2]
> Whistle
> Waterproof match container with
>   matches
> Tourniquet
> Cravat[3]
> Two pressure dressings

When we had checked all the items and repacked them in the canister, a new man appeared and took charge of the formation. He identified himself as Major Odessa, the commander of the Selection detachment. He was a medium-sized man with sandy hair and a close-cropped mustache. His skin was the color of light rust. He had the unassuming appearance of someone who would not be singled out in a

[1] Red smoke is for danger.
[2] Purple smoke is for showing location.
[3] A cravat can be used for a sling or a tourniquet.

crowd. But there was an inner power to him that could be felt from a distance and seen in his eyes.

"Now that the preliminaries are out of the way and some of the less-determined individuals have departed for home, we can get down to business," he announced.

"For the next several weeks you will undergo the selection process for acceptance into the First Special Forces Operational Detachment–Delta. Despite the name, this is not a Special Forces unit. It neither belongs to nor reports to the Special Forces Command.[4] This is a new organization whose sole purpose is to perform counterterrorist and other special operations as directed by the National Command Authority.[5]

"This is not a training course. It is a selection course. Those who are accepted will be trained once they are assigned to the unit.

"Now some ground rules. They are simple and few. Everything you see, hear, and do during this course is classified. You will keep it to yourself. Everything you will do is an individual effort. That means you will assist no other Selection candidate and you will accept assistance from no one whatsoever.

"You are all seasoned soldiers, and experienced NCOs, and officers. So we know that each of you can operate as a member, and as a leader, of a team. But that isn't our concern. We want to know how you operate as an individual. The vehicle we will use to assess that is cross-country navigation or, as the civilians call it, orienteering.

---

[4] "Chain of command" refers to the way both individuals and units report in the military. Delta was set up to report directly to the Pentagon to make it as nimble as possible.

[5] National Command Authority is the president and his security advisors.

"Each day you will receive the instructions necessary to get you started. As you go along, you will receive the instructions you need for the next event, much as you have received to this point.

"You will carry a prescribed load between designated rendezvous points or, as we call them, RVs. Upon arrival at a new point, you will receive new instructions from the cadre member manning that point. You will have finished the day when a cadre member tells you to take off your rucksack and sit down."

We were riveted to his words. No one moved a muscle as he spoke.

"You will be operating against a time standard, but you will not know what that standard is. However, you will be given an 'overdue' time at the start of every day. If you are not at an RV point at that time, you will move to the nearest road and sit down where you can be seen. The cadre will begin looking for you at the overdue time.

"If you become lost to the point that you cannot find a road at overdue time, or you become injured and can no longer go on, use your emergency signaling kit. If you have a life- or limb-threatening injury, use the radio. If night has arrived and you have not been found, build and maintain a small fire in the largest clearing or open area you can find. We will be searching for you, and you will be found.

"As you move from RV to RV, you will stay off all roads and trails. We define a road or trail as a path currently capable of jeep traffic. If you find that your route is running parallel to a road or trail, you will stay at least fifteen meters away. You may walk on a road or trail for the fifteen meters approaching or departing an RV.

"If you become injured or sick and require medical attention, tell the nearest cadre member, 'I require medical attention.'

"If for any reason, at any time, you no longer desire to continue with the Selection course, tell any cadre member, 'I wish to voluntarily withdraw from the course.' No one will question your decision. You will be immediately withdrawn and returned to your parent unit.

"No course reports will be filed on you and neither you nor we will talk about anything that takes place during this course. Is there anything I've said to this point that is unclear?"

Amazingly, there were no questions from anyone.

"Then we will begin," continued the major. "Remember, you are competing against an unannounced time standard. You are not competing against one another. You will receive the instructions you need to complete each event. Add nothing to the instructions. Subtract nothing from the instructions. Read nothing into the instructions that is not stated.

"The cadre will not assist you, and you will not assist one another or accept any outside assistance. This is an individual effort. Willful failure to follow instructions will result in dismissal from the course. Failure to meet Selection standards will result in dismissal from the course.

"Do your utmost at all times, and you may find that to be sufficient." He finished his presentation, then looked at us once more before turning us over to a cadre member and silently departing.

We were then instructed to fall out in thirty minutes with a forty-pound rucksack, emergency kit packed inside, a compass, and one C ration meal. At formation, we were each given a color and number as our individual identification code and a map sheet of Fort Bragg.

We were assigned to trucks by color and number. I couldn't detect any pattern in the assignments. Normal army method would be to put all "reds" on one truck, all "blues" on another, and all "greens" on yet another. Or at least, if mixing color groups, the numbers would run in sequence. The arbitrariness of this was obviously purposeful.

Our convoy of trucks moved out of the compound and scattered in all directions as soon as we hit the road. Some went left and some went right; one moved straight across the highway and stopped. As our group continued on, a truck would turn off here or there until we, too, pulled off onto a sand trail and eventually came to a stop in a choking cloud of dust.

The driver opened the tailgate, and a cadre member told us to dismount but stay on the other side of the truck until he called us forward, four at a time, each with a different color.

I was in the first group called forward, and as we approached, the cadre pointed out a spot for each color and told us we would find our instructions on a sheet of paper at our spot.

I moved to the place he indicated, a large persimmon tree about twenty meters away, and found an acetate-covered sheet of paper tacked to the base of it. The sheet was marked with my color and had a set of map coordinates for that location.

It also said, "Your next RV is located at... ," and gave the eight-digit grid coordinates for that point. Below that was printed the overdue time for the day.

I sat on my rucksack and transposed both sets of coordinates, marked each location on the map, and wrote the overdue time in the green army pocket notebook I always carried in my shirt pocket. I took out my compass, oriented the map, and was studying the possible routes and calculating distances when the cadre member called me to his location.

"Open your map, show me where you are, and show me where you're going," he instructed in a flat, matter-of-fact tone.

I picked up a twig from the ground and, using it as a pointer, said, "I am here and am going there," pointing to each location in turn with the twig.

"OK," he replied, and looked into my face with a deadpan stare. "Have a good 'un."

I made no reply; I just nodded, shouldered my rucksack, took my initial compass bearing, and set out on the first steps into the unknown.

I picked a pace that, given this terrain and the offsets of my route, should move me to my destination at about five kilometers an hour. It was a pace that covered ground well enough but was also one I could maintain with the load I was carrying for a long, long time. I had to move fast without burning myself out, because I didn't have any idea when I would finish.

That initial leg was about six kilometers. Along the way I saw one or two other guys scurrying down different routes. We studiously ignored each other and continued on our respective paths.

The day was warm, but not hot, and the air was dry. There was even a little bit of a breeze blowing as I crossed the tops of the broad low hills. The ruck was settled on my back, and I soon worked up a good sweat.

There were no land mines. No one was shooting artillery or machine guns at me. I had no one to worry about other than myself. I was healthy, strong, and moving well on a new adventure. All in all, a pretty good day.

I was getting close to the RV. I had marked the location at a slight bend of a sand trail that contoured about halfway up a small hill. I saw the point when I was about twenty-five meters out. As I closed with it, the RV sitter saw me and called, "Color and number."

I responded with my code for the day, and the sitter replied, "Roger, green six. Your instructions are over there," and he pointed to one of the sheets posted about the area. "Water is on the back of the truck. Come and see me when you're ready," he said as he scribbled something on a clipboard.

I nodded and moved to my instruction sheet. All it said was "GREEN: Your next RV is located at . . . ," and it gave the eight-digit coordinates of the new location.

I plotted the spot on the map and reported to the sitter.

"Show me where you are and show me where you're going," he directed.

I did so, received the inevitable "Have a good 'un," and moved out sharply on the new route.

The rest of the day was much the same. The legs between RVs were four to seven kilometers in length. The terrain was consistent except for one good-sized creek I had to wade across. Occasionally, I would cross paths with other candidates, but otherwise I was alone. It was a good workout, vigorous, but not overly demanding.

My only apprehension was whether I was moving fast enough. But I knew this was a good pace. I was covering ground quickly, and my navigation was accurate. I *could* go faster if I had to, but that raised the risk of getting hurt or becoming overfatigued, and of my navigation becoming sloppy.

I arrived at my sixth RV in the late afternoon and called out my color and number as soon as the sitter looked up at my approach.

"Roger, Green Six. Go across the road to those pines, take off your rucksack, and sit down." He pointed to a clump of pines about thirty meters away.

I stood there uncertainly for a second and asked, "Am I finished?"

He merely repeated, "Go across the road to those pines, take off your rucksack, and sit down." He said it in a level, calm voice, as if I had never caused him to repeat his statement. No exasperation, no snideness, no emphasis, just the statement of instructions.

"Right," I said as I moved away. *Just do as you're told and don't ask questions unless the instructions are unclear.*

I crossed the street and shucked off my rucksack. It felt good to get that weight off my back. A person can become accustomed to carrying a ruck, but it never becomes comfortable. I plucked my canteens from their covers, drained the last one down my throat, and filled them both from one of the water cans nearby. Then I sat down and leaned back against my ruck, propped my feet up a tree, and thought about the day as I sipped a canteen.

This must be the finish point for the day and I must be doing OK, I thought. *I'm the only one here, so I must be first. No, maybe I'm late and a truckful has already gone in. No, that can't be right; to get here faster than I did, you'd have to run all day.*

But maybe the others didn't come from my starting point; maybe they came from other points and had different legs, maybe. . . . The heck with it! I don't know and I'm not going to worry about it or waste energy trying to figure it out. I'll just do my best and if that's not good enough, they can send me home.

But within a few minutes, another guy showed up at the RV and came over to the rest spot under the pines. I had not seen him before now. We introduced ourselves as he dropped his ruck and settled down.

His name was Ron Cardowski, and he was a tall, lean master sergeant stationed with the Tenth Special Forces in Bad Tölz, Germany. Bad Tölz is one of my favorite places, and I have many friends stationed there, so we chatted about mutual acquaintances and favorite ski slopes as more candidates began to arrive at our location.

After a half hour or so, there were about fifteen men lounging in the shade of the pine grove. A little later, a deuce-and-a-half pulled up and the RV sitter told us to climb aboard. One guy had to ask if the truck was going back to camp, and he seemed a little put out when the sitter merely repeated, "Get on the truck." The guy climbed aboard, muttering to himself.

As the truck bounced along the dusty sand trail, I retreated into myself and thought about that guy, about my question of "Am I finished?" and other things I had noticed. The factor of the unknown was subtly but persistently at work here.

The army lives and operates by published schedules. In peacetime, the document that regulates life is the unit training schedule. The training schedule is published weekly and announces each day's agenda in detail: time of formations, hourly activities, uniform requirements, classes and the names of the instructors, activity locations, mealtimes and what type of rations are provided, special notes, and what time the duty day ends. Other notices, such as the duty roster,[6] round out these detailed instructions.

For field and combat operations, the operations order provides all the instructions for the conduct of foreseen activities. As most people suspect, military life is a highly regulated affair. And for experienced soldiers, that amount of regulation gives a certain sense of comfort. It provides the framework they need to plan, conduct, and pursue their duties and their lives. The inevitable changes wrought on the training schedule—just because all things cannot be minutely regulated—always produce some degree of turmoil in a unit.

So you can imagine the effect this minimal instruction was having on everyone in the Selection course. We were all affected to varying degrees. I have always prided myself on my adaptability and my capacity for overcoming obstacles, but I could feel anxiety about the unknowns of this course hovering in the back of my mind.

What was going to happen next? Was I moving fast enough? How long was it all going to last? Were there "spies" in the course, watching, listening, and reporting back to the cadre? I thought about these things and others on the truck ride and came to the conclusion that I didn't care about any of them. The factor of the unknown was exhilarating, and I enjoyed it.

---

[6] The duty roster is a list and schedule showing who handles any type of recurring duty, such as guard duty or KP.

But one of us had reached a different conclusion by the time our truck arrived back at camp. He was a well-built, tough-looking sergeant first class serving on drill sergeant duty with a basic training brigade. When we piled off the truck, he went to the cadre member standing nearby and reported that he wished to voluntarily withdraw from the course. Those of us present were surprised to see it happen; this guy was no slouch. The cadre member merely directed him to the orderly room for out-processing and then told the rest of us that instructions were on the bulletin board.

Word filtered out later that he had told Sergeant Major Shumate he was packing it in because he couldn't stand not knowing what he would be doing—not just after the next event, but the next day and the day after that. He said he realized that he required structure and organization and that this just wasn't for him. I never saw him again.

Later that evening, they showed a movie in the mess hall. *Marathon Man*.

The next six days were much like the first one. Point to point, I covered just about the entire western half of Fort Bragg. Every day we had a different color and number, and every day we started and finished with a different group.

Some days there were fewer RVs to hit, but the legs were longer and more difficult. Other days there were more RVs, and once, I was nearing the overdue time when I finally finished. The end of some days found as many as twenty of us at the final RV, but on another day, only four of us got on the same truck back to camp.

Cadre members would show up for a day and then disappear.

But no matter who they were, the RV sitters always acted the same, with a calm, deliberate, dispassionate, "Just the facts, ma'am" demeanor. We never saw any of them get ruffled or have the slightest flutter in their composure. They didn't smile; they didn't frown; and they didn't gesture. But they always watched.

Everything happened when it was supposed to. If the bulletin board announced truck departure at 0600 hours, trucks rolled at 0600. If someone missed the trucks, he was never seen or spoken of again. The steady disappearance of men was downright eerie. Every night the crowd in the mess hall got smaller. No one saw them leave; no one heard them leave; they were just . . . gone.

The Midnight Hook, as we called the mechanism behind these vanishing acts, had already snatched three old comrades of mine.

Day seven was a very short day. We returned to camp at 1300 hours and headed straight to the classroom for another round of psychological testing. It felt peculiar, sitting at a school desk, dog tired and soaked through with sweat, methodically taking a written examination, knowing we'd never see the results. All we'd be able to do was wonder if we had passed, failed, or fallen somewhere in between.

There was a formation that evening after chow. Major Odessa, the Iron Major, as I thought of him, was in charge.

"Men, this last week has been a practice session. Some of you have been away from tactical units[7] for a while and needed to hone your navigational skills. Some men, who have since departed, didn't really want to be here and just

---

[7] Tactical units: units that go to combat.

needed a little time to realize that fact. Up until now, the only men who have returned to their units have been those too injured to carry on or those who have voluntarily withdrawn from the course. That all changes tomorrow."

Holding himself perfectly still, he paused, as if gathering his thoughts. I held my breath and felt myself freeze along with him. Then he continued, and I breathed again.

"Tomorrow you begin Stress Phase. You will be relocating to a remote mountainous field location. You will be camping in the open. Prepare for a ten-day stay in the field and pack your duffel bag accordingly. All meals will be C rations. Potable water will be provided; do not drink from any streams or other bodies of water.

"After this formation, you will report to the supply room to draw a weapon and the map sheets you will need. Keep those items with you at all times. You will carry your weapon in your hand; they do not have slings attached, and you will not rig a sling or tie the weapon to your body.

"Replace or draw any additional equipment you need this evening. Pack anything you will not need for the field and store it in the supply room. Privately owned vehicles will stay here.

"As of tomorrow, your movement between RVs will be timed, and you will be judged against a set time standard for movement. Do not worry yourself trying to determine what that time standard is. Just do the best you can.

"There are those of you here now who will fail to meet course standards and will be removed from the Selection course for that failure. Those men will be returned to their units with a copy of a letter that will go to their commanding officer declaring that man to be both an exemplary soldier and a credit to his unit, but not, unfortunately, selected for service with this unit at this time. Indeed, all of you are excellent soldiers or you would not still be here.

"Things have been rather easy until now. The difficulty will increase tomorrow. Pay attention, follow instructions, and do your best. That's all we require.

"Since there are no questions, you are released to prepare for tomorrow. Additional instructions are posted on the bulletin board. Have a good 'un." And with that, the major turned on his heel and walked out of the room.

You mean I've been walking for fun this whole last week? I thought. But I knew I'd profited from the past seven days of practice. My navigation was razor sharp, my conditioning was even better, and I was becoming accustomed to being on my own and not having a forty-four-man platoon to shepherd about.

But it wasn't all freedom. The cadre had been watching and keeping notes on us all along—and not just our RV times. They weren't sneaky about it, but neither were they very open. If we paid attention, we could see that they observed everything going on and that they would sometimes write in a notebook before continuing with whatever they were doing.

Some guys were really agitated by it and worried about what was being recorded in those notes. I thought that the observation reports were genuine, but that some of the note-taking was designed purely to create anxiety. I later found this to be true.

I checked the bulletin board for instructions and headed

for the supply room. Sergeant Major Shumate was standing nearby, smoking a cigarette and watching the sunset.

I greeted him as I walked past. "Evening, Sergeant Major."

He was holding his cigarette at arm's length and squinting at it with one eye as if trying to detect some defect.

"Hey there, Ranger," he said, looking up. "Still hanging around, eh? It must be that you like the chow . . . 'cause there sure ain't no booze or women here 'bouts."

The cigarette must have passed inspection, because he reeled it in and took an elaborate draw while eyeing me from beneath his brows, and that amused smile I had seen before lifted the ends of his mustache.

"I guess that's it, Sergeant Major, and besides, I've been needing a little vacation anyway."

He snorted in reply as he exhaled through his nose, then with elegant grace blew a slow, rolling ring into the still air. "A lot of these guys wouldn't know what you mean by that," he said, glancing around the yard. "But I remember what it's like to be a platoon sergeant, and I think it was easier back then than it is now. So yeah, enjoy what you can; none of this lasts forever. Maybe I'll see you when you get back," he said in dismissal.

"I hope so, Sergeant Major."

"Yeah," he replied, and returned his attention to the sunset and his cigarette.

I glanced back as I opened the door to the supply room. From where I stood, he looked like a man surveying the universe from some secret vantage point.

Maybe he was.

CHAPTER**FOUR**

Somewhere in the
Uwharrie Mountains

The Uwharries are an eruption of rugged terrain about fifty miles northwest of Fort Bragg. A quick study of the map sheets told me the land was not gentle. In fact, it looked very similar to the Appalachian Ridge and Valley region, where I had grown up in north Georgia.

We had mounted up early for the ride to our new location. I'd thought we would set up camp first, but a couple of hours into the trip, our convoy started to break up, and pretty soon our truck was traveling alone. We turned onto a narrow paved road and then came to a halt. A cadre member called us off the truck four at a time. I was itching to get going and glad to be in the first group.

The RV sitter was a cadre member named Carlos. He sent me around to the front of his vehicle, an old bread delivery van, to read the instructions posted on the hood of the truck.

The weapon I had been issued was a grease gun, the old

.45-caliber submachine gun that had been army standard since the Second World War. It was reliable, but very heavy for its size, and awkward to carry, particularly without a sling. I tried to lay it on the hood of the truck as I plotted the coordinates on my map, but it kept sliding off. I didn't want to lay it on the ground because the grass was wet from a heavy dew. After looking around for a decent place to put it, I stuck it, barrel first, into the grill of the truck and let it dangle there.

I took my map over to Carlos, showed him where I was and where I was going, slung my rucksack onto my back, and hauled butt out of the RV on my initial heading.

This was it—the first leg of the first real day—and I was fired up. I felt so strong my feet barely touched the ground as I left the RV. As soon as I crossed the road, I had to negotiate a barbed-wire fence on the other side. But that was no problem. I threw my right hand on top of a fence post and bounded over in one great leap, and while in midair over the fence, I saw my empty left hand.

Oh, man. I left my weapon at the RV. I hit the ground on the far side of the fence with the exhilaration hissing out of me like air from a punctured beach ball. Carlos watched me all the way back to the truck, where I sheepishly pulled my weapon from the grill and departed, this time at a more moderate pace.

His dispassionate "Have a good 'un" stung like a shotgun blast of rock salt, particularly when I realized that he hadn't said it on my first departure. He knew I was screwing up all along but had given no hint of it.

Well, it was a good lesson. My pride was bruised a little, and I'd lost a few minutes. I'd probably even gotten a notation of "Bonehead Attack" beside my name in Carlos' notebook. I'd make a point of not letting it happen again.

The terrain here was much more difficult to negotiate than that on Fort Bragg, but I felt I needed to cover just as much ground per hour as before. I would have to be smarter in my route selection, because I wouldn't be able to beat down the mountains. If I tried to assault them, eventually they would overpower me. Or better said, I would over-power myself bashing against them. All I wanted was their indifference. In return, I promised the mountains I would make my passage as unobtrusive as I could.

My routes the first day seemed positively screwy. From RV to RV, I found myself contouring clockwise, midway up the slopes of various ridges. I wanted to cross their spines, where I could get on their tops and run the long axis. But on every leg, doing that would have carried me so far out of the way as to not be worth the effort. A waste of precious energy. I spent the majority of my time on the slopes going in wide circles with my left foot downhill. It was so continuous that I got one of the few foot blisters I'd ever had in my life—on the outside of my left foot, the perpetually downhill side.

I saw only one other person between RVs that day. Sometime in the afternoon I came across Captain Jim Bush limping along.

Jim had also come to Selection from First Ranger. He had commanded our company until earlier in the year, and since that time, he had been serving as the assistant opera-tions officer for the Battalion, a job he didn't particularly care for. Jim was one of those hard-core combat officers who prefer to be in the field with the troops. And though staff positions are important, they naturally rub a man such as Captain Bush the wrong way. He was also as tough as shoe leather—and if he was limping, he was hurt pretty badly. Still, Jim Bush could limp faster than most men could walk.

I broke the code of silence and asked him what had happened as our paths crossed.

"Caught my foot between two rocks coming down the slope of a mountain and twisted my ankle. Didn't hear or feel anything crack, so I'm hoping it's just a sprain. I'll know tonight when I pull the boot off," he said between compressed lips and gritted teeth.

"OK, Cap'n. See you later." And we continued on our separate ways.

Luck. Pure luck was going to play its part in this endeavor. The luck not to fall and break a leg, the luck not to get a stick jammed in the eye, the luck not to be bitten by a snake or to do something so stupid that I couldn't recover from it. Luck is always in the mix, and I just hoped to avoid the bad side of it.

To help that, I had brought my best talisman with me.

It wasn't anything special—just the jungle fatigues I was wearing. They had become good luck through use. I had worn the same set every day so far and would continue to wear them as long as their luck held up, no matter how rank they became.

I had brought three sets of fatigues with me to Selection. One set was in reserve; one set I wore in the evenings, after cleaning up from the days' activities; and the other set I wore every day. They weren't as ripe as you might think. I had already washed them out once or twice and hung them up at night. In the mornings, they were no more wet than when I had taken them off, soaked in sweat, the evening before. They had accumulated luck, and luck attracts more luck. And I didn't want to do anything that might break the cycle.

Late in the afternoon I was finally told to drop ruck and sit down. Again I was by myself until, within minutes, another candidate, Ron, joined me at the finish point. It had been a tough day and I was bushed. Our load had been increased by five pounds, and my feet and knees were tired and sore from contouring in the same position all day.

Within thirty minutes we were joined by about a half dozen more men. I could hear other men being sent to another location about fifty meters away on the other side of the road. Two trucks pulled up at the RV, and a cadre member came over and told our group to get on the first one. We grabbed our rucks and climbed aboard.

As the truck rumbled off, I looked at the other group, but they were still sitting there. I wondered which of us was going where, then quickly dismissed the thought. The men in the other group weren't my concern, and as for me, I'd know the destination when I got there. This was an exercise in dealing with the unknown. And liking it.

We rode for about a half hour and then pulled up into a logging road. Several men were called off, and the rest of us continued along. At a second stop, I was called off the truck with four or five other men. Marvin was waiting there for us. He had been the sitter at my second RV that day. As soon as we dismounted, he gave us our instructions.

"This is where you'll make camp tonight. Your bags are on the back of my truck. So are water and C rations. Stay in a group within twenty-five meters of the truck. Fires are authorized but must be doused by 2200 hours; keep them small and under control. The medic will be here later if anyone needs to see him. Scales are slung in front of the truck. Rucksack weight for tomorrow is fifty pounds. You will receive your color and number for the day at 0545. The vehicle departure time in the morning is 0600. . . . Don't be late and don't be light." And with that he focused his attention on his clipboard.

I nabbed my bag and looked for a good spot between two trees to set up a poncho hooch. I was almost finished when another truck pulled up and dropped off a half dozen more men, who received the same briefing from Marvin. I paid little attention to the new arrivals until Virg Parks brayed in my ear.

"Hey, bud, that looks like a good spot you got there. I'll just join you!" he shouted from a foot away. Parks always stood as close to someone as possible, as if he was going to whisper some intimate secret, and then hollered as though he was calling hogs. He threw his kit bag and rucksack in a heap on the ground and started digging through his pockets. I knew what was coming next.

"Hey, bud, ya got a cigarette?" he asked, rooting through his pockets for what he knew wasn't there.

"No, Parks, I quit smoking. It got too expensive supporting my habit *and* people like you," I replied as I got a clean set of jungle fatigues out of my kit bag. It was no joke. Parks was the biggest mooch I'd seen in my life.

"Well . . . ," Parks began, eyeing my poncho hooch and planting a just-found cigarette in his mouth. "I'll just tie my poncho to yours and we'll make one big hooch. Got some more of that suspension line?"

71

"Sure, Parks. Here." I handed him a few feet of cord. Then I moved away a bit to give myself a canteen cup bath, shave, change clothes, and hang up my lucky uniform to dry and air out.

The following morning at 0600 hours, the trucks rolled as promised. I was glad to get moving out of the first RV. My legs were a little stiff and my uniform was still damp and cold, but both discomforts would rapidly go away.

What a day. I was moving right at the ragged edge of my capability. Every route to every RV was a struggle. The drift of the land was contrary to every one of my routes. I was never able to use a valley or a ridge to advantage. Every slope was rocky, rugged, and covered with deadfall. The low ground was worse—a tangle of vines and briars. We called them "wait a minute" vines, because whenever someone got tangled up in them, his buddies would be waiting for him to get out. Whoever had laid out that day's course had done so with studied devilment in mind. It was impossible to maintain good time, and I was worried about being too slow.

I was bashing along a wide, relatively flat spot on the side of a slope when I came across an old abandoned farmstead. The place was overgrown with brush and blackberry briars, but right in the middle of what had been the front yard, I found a bush full of ripe Tommy Toe tomatoes. The Tommy Toe is a perennial plant, and that bush had been dropping fruit here for no telling how many years.

I stopped for the few seconds it took to fill the cargo pockets of my fatigue pants and took off again, popping those sweet and juicy little tomatoes into my mouth one right after the other. What an unexpected and uplifting treat.

The day became even rougher. The slopes were so steep that, even tracking back and forth, I had to pull myself from tree to tree to reach the top. The descents were even more hazardous. One misplaced step, one slip, one leaf-covered stump hole or slick tree root and that would be it.

As the day wore on, I started to get worried. It was less than thirty minutes until overdue time, and I was still more than a kilometer from my next RV. I poured on my reserves of energy and picked up my pace. I hustled into the RV with about five minutes to spare, shouting my color and number as soon as I saw the sitter.

He consulted his watch, jotted down my info, told me to hang my ruck on the scales at the RV, and pointed to one of the sheets of acetate paper situated around the area. "Come see me when you're ready," he said.

I hung my rucksack on the scales and went to plot my next RV. *I'm screwed now. There's no way I can get to the next RV with, what, two minutes left until overdue time? Why didn't I move faster? Why didn't I pick better routes?* I'd moved as hard as I could. I'd picked the best routes I could figure. It just wasn't going to be good enough. I reported to the sitter.

He glanced up as I started to spread my map and go through the drill. "Take your ruck off the scales and go sit by that big rock," he said, gesturing to the other side of the clearing.

I looked into his eyes briefly for a clue as to how I had done, but saw no hint of information. "OK," I replied as I hoisted my rucksack off the hook and went to the place he had indicated. *Man*, I thought as I sat down and propped my feet up. *If I've screwed this day up, Superman himself would have had a tough time.*

I sat there sipping water and studying the routes I had taken that day. No, I wasn't able to see how I could have picked better routes. And even though the routes had been more difficult that day, I had still managed to make what I considered to be good time. But if that wasn't good enough, I was in trouble.

Within the next half hour, other guys came rushing into the RV, sweat-soaked, uniforms ripped and torn, faces splotched red from exertion. They all received the same treatment I had, and each of them eyed me quizzically when he saw me sitting down, apparently finished, while he plotted his next RV.

The fourth man to come into the position stared longingly at the three of us sitting together on the far side of the clearing when the sitter told him to hang his ruck on the scale and move to his instruction sheet. He just stood there, shoulders slumped, chest heaving, and hands at his sides. After a short pause, he took a ragged breath and said, "I voluntarily withdraw."

The sitter replied, "Take your rucksack and move over there, down the slope, and sit down," and pointed to a position that would be out of sight of the RV.

The poor guy stumbled away and out of sight. He never looked back. Our little cluster kept our mouths shut and only lifted eyebrows at one another in communication.

What was the lesson here? Simple. Don't quit. Never quit, no matter what. Keep going until someone tells you to sit down. Keep going as long as you're able to move, no matter how poorly you think you may be doing. Just don't quit.

Camp that night was in another location with a completely different group of men. We received the same instructions as we had the evening before and settled in for a night's rest. But that evening, the medic had a number of visitors when he stopped by on his rounds.

Next day: more of the same, only worse.

Long grueling legs over terrain never lending itself to route selection. I was never able to plot a route that approximated a line between RVs. To use the terrain to any sort of advantage, I had to make lung-busting climbs upslope to top a long ridge that would carry me only vaguely in the direction of the next RV. There was simply no margin for error. But the more tired I got, the more difficult it became not to make mistakes.

About midafternoon, things got hectic. I had just dropped off a ridgetop and was zeroing in on my RV when I was overrun by civilians blasting through the woods on cross-country motorcycles.

There were dozens of them all over the place, motors squalling like angry hornets. I felt like a slow ship with kamikazes buzzing about me. They seemed to be going in the same general direction that I was taking—up a broad but rapidly narrowing hollow to a pass in the mountain called Gold Mine Branch.

Just as I came in sight of the RV, a motorbike whipped past me with a passenger wearing a rucksack holding on to the rider. Yep, that's right . . . a Selection candidate.

The bike stopped next to the RV sitter's truck, and as

the candidate got off the back of the bike, I heard him say to the sitter, "I reckon that was a little too far, eh?"

"Put your ruck in the back of my truck and make yourself comfortable. A vehicle will pick you up shortly," said the sitter.

The guy turned back to the biker he had hitched the ride with and told him with a wave, "Thanks for the lift, man. I'll catch you later," then threw his rucksack in the truck and sat on the bumper while the biker blasted out of the RV in a shower of dirt and leaves.

Wow! That was some kind of a championship screwup. I plotted my next RV and looked the guy in the face as I walked toward the sitter. He threw up his hands with a shrug and a grin that said, "Ah, what the heck, I tried."

I grinned back at him and shook my head as I walked by. I watched the sitter closely as we went through the departure ritual. If Easy Rider had surprised him or upset his equilibrium, I wasn't able to detect it.

And so another guy went into Delta Force legend. Even now, when we old hands get together and talk about Selection and the things we've seen over the years, someone will inevitably say, "Remember that guy who came into the RV on the back of a motorcycle?" Fellow, whoever you are, I want you to know that your place in history is secure. Somehow, I think you'll be pleased.

The rest of the day passed in a sweat-blurred flurry of upslope, downslope, and traverse slope. Of heaving chest, burning lungs, quivering legs, and aching back. Of terrain-feature counting, pace count, and compass sightings. My body was drenched in sweat; my face and hands were cut and scratched by sticks, briars, and thorns. Eventually it came to an end. When I finally sat down, I felt like a toothpaste tube that had been squeezed empty. It was an effort to throw my rucksack aboard the truck and climb up after it.

We departed that final RV differently that day. Instead of our group getting on the same truck, we were called individually by color and number and sent to several different trucks.

A question immediately arose in my mind—and doubtless in the minds of the other men. *Is this truck taking me to camp or is this truck going back to Fort Bragg?* The question was answered when we were dropped off at a new campsite. *All right,* I thought. *I'll be here at least one more day.*

Camp was unusually quiet that evening. The rule of no conversation during the day had seeped into camp as well.

Daylight and at it again on another tremendously difficult day. Agonizing climbs upslope followed by hazardous descents.

To go downslope without sliding out of control, you have to lean forward, putting the weight of your upper body downhill and over your feet, much like while skiing. But if you trip in that position, your rucksack will drive you face-first into the ground or a tree—and with nothing to cushion the fall, you may not recover.

I had taken a few falls already, but each time, I had been able to twist around and fall on my side so that my rucksack wasn't on top of me when I hit the ground. So far, my luck was holding.

Throughout the morning and into midday, I saw no other candidates between RVs. It was as if I had the mountains to myself. By late in the afternoon, I was tracking along the top of a long narrow ridge that, for once, was taking me in the direction of my next RV.

Earlier, I had gone almost a half kilometer out of the way to gain the top of this ridge by way of a long sloping finger offering a somewhat gradual route up the otherwise precipitous sides. But it had paid off. I was making excellent time by virtue of the energy I had saved.

Then I heard a human voice. Not a conversational voice, but the voice of someone wailing in deathlike agony. It was coming from just ahead and off the side of the ridge. I trotted to a place where I could see down the mountain slope and spotted him a hundred meters below. He was midway up the steepest portion of the whole mountain, hauling himself tree to tree and rock to rock up what could only be described as a cliff—just to lose his grip and slide back again. He was yelling as if he was being disemboweled with a rusty file. I watched him for a few seconds, then shook my head in wonder and moved on. The sounds of his battle faded behind me as I continued on my trek. I never saw that man again.

With the sun slipping low in the western sky, my day finally and mercifully ended. A new camp location, a different group of guys, a couple of familiar faces. I didn't bother to count heads, but the camp population was decidedly shrinking.

I slept like the dead that night, and if I dreamed, I never knew it.

I didn't realize it when I set out that morning, but I was going to become intimately familiar with the topography[1] of

---

[1] The features of a piece of land.

Gold Mine Branch. The day would become known as the "Day of the Star," because when drawn on a map, the routes formed a six-pointed star.

All day long, I crossed that mountain from one side to the other. On the map the mountain looked like a big, dead, contorted octopus. The main body was lumpy and irregular; the top writhed tentacle-like in a series of sharp-crested saddles. The fingers and ridges running off the sides of the crest were gnarled and twisted like the arthritic hands of an old man.

I would arrive exhausted and breathless at one RV only to be sent to the next RV back on the side I had just come from. The mountain was too big to contour around, and the lay of the ground was such that I could never make anything approximating a direct approach or maintain the hard-earned high ground for any length of time. Never getting anywhere, back and forth across the same mountain. It was a masterful torture. But then I had a revelation.

What difference could it possibly make if I crossed back and forth over this mountain until doomsday?

A mountain was a mountain, time was time, and route selection was route selection. The only thing that mattered was speed and ground made good. My destination was determined by time; the physical position of that ultimate destination was only incidental to my reason for being there. The frustration and mental torture I had been suffering were completely of my own making—and completely within my power to disregard.

I dropped all thoughts of anything other than making the best possible approach to the next RV, and it was amazing how much stronger I felt mentally and physically.

From then on, it was just a hard day in the mountains. And as happens with all days, no matter how difficult, this one, too, came to a close. I finished the day at RV Easy Rider, the spot where Biker Boy had brought his Selection to such a notable conclusion.

Eventually about twenty of us had arrived and were sitting in one group instead of the usual two or three widely separated clusters. After the trucks came and went, I was left sitting with only six or seven other guys. What was the significance of this?

Before long, a truck arrived with our bags and we were told to make camp right there. A few minutes later, another truck arrived and dropped off three or four more men.

I didn't know it until later, but that was the day of the Big Cut. Those who had collected enough late points against them got the axe at the end of that day. This winnowing of the harvest had brought us down to about 30 men—30 out of the original 163 who had started out the first day back at Aberdeen Camp.

I've talked about the unknown or unannounced time standard of the Selection course. After going through Selection, and later working as a cadre member of Selection, I'm still not sure what the time standard is. The only people who know for certain are the Selection detachment commander and the noncommissioned officer in charge (NCOIC).

No one else is privy to that information. Not even the Delta Force commander himself. It is one of the best-kept, most well-compartmentalized secrets in the Western world. It ensures that no candidate, even those who have to come back for a subsequent try, will ever have an advantage over anyone else.

Every man who ultimately makes it through Delta Selection has had to gauge his performance by his own internal yardstick. He's had to give his utmost because he couldn't be sure just how good was good enough. It keeps everyone honest.

The evening in camp passed in a leisurely fashion. A small group of us sat around talking about our different units, the army, politics, and national events. That evening I also realized something: we had started the course with an average complement of pro football player–sized men, but most of those had disappeared after the eighteen-miler. And the two or three who had started Stress Phase were now missing in action.

As I looked around at my camp mates and thought about the men I had seen in the past couple of days, it hit me that every man here was more or less average. All shapes, sizes, and builds—but no massive men. A few big guys made it into the unit, but they were greatly outnumbered by men of below-average size.

Selection taxed all our abilities, mental and physical. The mountains would win if we took them head-on, so we had to outthink them. But craftiness alone wouldn't get us from RV to RV on time, much less allow us to keep it up day after day. That required superior physical conditioning, but conditioning and tenacity is not dependent upon size alone. Only a tough body coupled with a tough mind bought a winning ticket to Selection. One without the other could not and would not succeed.

The next day held the easiest ground I had crossed so far. The slopes were still high and steep, but the terrain was even and regular. The trees were big mature hardwoods with very little underbrush. The ground was smooth, with few rocks. It was a place to make good time. And I was taking advantage of it, because I was certain that conditions would change very soon. They did.

I was pushing along toward my next RV when I came across a twelve-foot-high chain-link fence stretching out of sight in each direction. The question was whether to go under it, over it, or around it.

I had a sneaking suspicion that I would encounter something worse if I attempted to go around the fence. Its skirt was anchored in the ground (probably as a barrier to wild hogs), and that prevented me from going under. That left going over the top. I'm a good climber, but I had an additional seventy pounds on my body and it wouldn't be easy.

Here's what I planned: I'd put my grease gun down the front of my shirt, then climb to the top of the fence and throw my rucksack to the other side. Then I would climb over and down with ease.

Here's how it played out: The climb up wasn't very difficult, but once on top, I discovered I would have to sit straddling the fence to take off the rucksack and let it drop to the ground. But the fence was slack and wobbly, so when I tried to slip the straps off my shoulders, I got to swaying back and forth until the weight of the rucksack pulled me off balance and over the other side.

I was hanging upside down, dangling by my left leg from the top of the fence. The grease gun had slid out the top of my shirt and popped me in the mouth, splitting my upper lip and loosening two teeth. That rucksack was dangling below my head, and it had my shoulders locked. I couldn't shake it loose or my leg would give way and I'd fall headfirst.

Ever so slowly, I worked my right hand over until I could find the quick-release tab on the left shoulder strap. *Let's see . . . it's upside down, so I have to pull it the other way.* As soon as that shoulder was free, the rucksack hurtled earthward and hit with a crash. Then I had to do a long sit-up to get to the top of the fence, right myself, free my leg, and climb down.

Both feet on the ground once more, I looked around, hoping no one had seen that little episode. Then I gave that treacherous rucksack a vicious kick, and with the metallic taste of blood in my mouth, I shouldered the brute and took off again.

I hit the top of the mountain and went into my RV with a rush. Carlos was the sitter, and he sent me on to the next stop. From there I was sent right back to Carlos and his RV. *What's going on now?* I thought. *A variation on the Day of the Star?*

Carlos pointed me toward a different set of instructions, but then changed his mind. "No, go over there and sit down," he directed.

Wow, I was finished for the day and it wasn't quite 1030. I went to the spot Carlos had indicated, still in broad view of the RV. I shucked the ruck off my back, dug out a C ration, propped my feet up on a tree, and leaned back to enjoy my brunch. I was reclined there, enjoying the good life, when Virgil Parks came crashing into the RV like a roller coaster car that had jumped the tracks. He saw me sitting there and stopped as if he had run into an invisible wall.

"What are you doing just sitting there?" he asked with an incredulous look on his face.

He obviously thought I had quit but didn't want to

believe his eyes. I decided to have a little fun. I hung my head and in a whining, self-pitying voice slurred, "This is it, Parks. . . . I'm finished. I . . . I . . . I can't go any further today. I've reached the end."

A furious look of disgust inflamed his face as he raised his grease gun menacingly and stalked toward me. "Why you, you . . ."

Carlos called him off, and it was the first time I'd seen a break in the stone-faced detachment of a cadre member. "Hey, you!" He barked Parks' color and number. "Get over here and worry about yourself. That man's finished for today and you're not."

Parks lowered his grease gun and looked at me with surprise as he turned away to check into the RV and get his new instructions.

"Dang!" he said as he walked past me when he departed the RV. "You're finished already? You must be hauling butt!"

"Have a good 'un, Parks." I grinned as I lifted a can of C ration peaches in salute. "Have a good 'un."

It was thirty minutes before anyone else came in to stay, but then, four or five men arrived at the RV almost simultaneously. Shortly thereafter a truck with a half dozen other men aboard came to pick us up and took us to a spot on Blewitt Falls Lake. Major Odessa was waiting for us, along with our bags. Another truck came in right behind us and dropped off its passengers. We numbered about twenty in all.

The major called us over to him.

"Short day today, men," he said, surveying the crowd. "I suggest you take this opportunity to apply soap and water to your bodies. Some of you are getting rather ripe. When you finish, I'll have further instructions."

I dug my shaving kit out of my bag, grabbed a bar of soap, shucked off my uniform and boots, and plunged into the lake. Man, did it ever feel good. I waded back to the bank, lathered up, and plunged back in again. I did that several more times and then just floated in the water, enjoying the sensation of weightlessness.

What a treat. We laughed, joked, and made the most of this unexpected break before climbing out and putting on clean uniforms. I felt like a million bucks. Once everyone was squared away, Major Odessa spoke to us again.

"Men, tomorrow is the big day: the forty-miler. Those who successfully complete the event will stay for a bit more testing and an interview by the commander's evaluation board. Those who fail to satisfactorily complete the event will be returned to their units. This is no time to slack off and no time to rest. Some of you are not doing so well and are hanging on by the skin of your teeth. I'd recommend that every one of you give tomorrow your utmost effort.

"Now, as it appears that the matters of hygiene have been completed, you will be taken into the town of Troy, where you can obtain something other than C rations for the noon meal. Take your instructions for the rest of the day from Marvin." With that, the major turned to walk away.

An old acquaintance, Frank Trout, and I were walking up the trail together toward the trucks and we passed close to Major Odessa, who was standing just inside the tree line, watching the group file past. As we got near, he leaned forward, pointed his finger at us, and whispered in a forcefully contained voice, "And you're two of them I was talking about!"

Startled, we looked at him as he spoke, but we kept walking. *Holy Toledo! Was that right? No . . . that had to be bull. He was just keeping up the guessing game. Yeah, that's it; he was just playing games. I'm doing OK. But what about Frank?* Frank looked pretty rattled.

Well, the next day would tell. The next day the fat lady would sing, after a forty-mile opera.

I pitched my kit bag and rucksack into the back of the baggage van and climbed aboard the truck to town. We went in to Troy and scattered about the few places where we could get a meal. I had a decent lunch at a small diner, but I just as soon would have gone straight to camp and had a C ration. Once I'm in the field, I don't like to break my field attitude until it's all over. But no harm done.

That evening we were issued eight different map sheets and instructions for an 0200 hours departure. I turned in as soon as I had folded my maps and readied my gear for the next day. I heard no conversation in the camp that night.

Eighteen of us left the final camp that morning. We arrived at the start point, the head of the Uwharrie Trail, at 0300, and after a few simple instructions, we were released at three-minute intervals.

Major Odessa had given the short briefing: Use of roads and trails was authorized until instructed otherwise. We were allowed to follow the Uwharrie Trail until it terminated and then were to take further instructions from the RV sitter at trail's end. The trail would split at a point designated on the map, and we were to take the branch marked as the new trail. Cadre members would be posted where the trail crossed any roads. Have a good 'un.

And off went the first man.

At least thirty minutes later, I was still leaning against my rucksack, drumming my heels on the ground and watching the other candidates depart. Just a handful of us were still sitting there in the dark, and I was anxious to get going. *Hurry up and call my color and number.* I should have relaxed and napped. I was the last man released from the start point.

Daylight was a couple of hours away and the night was moonless, but I could feel the clear, hard-packed trail beneath my feet. It wasn't hard to follow and I didn't need to use a flashlight. That would just ruin my night vision, anyway. The chill air felt good rushing past my face, and since I was on the trail, I dropped my compass into a breast pocket of my jungle shirt instead of letting it dangle and bounce against my chest, where it normally hung from its lanyard.

Move hard while it's cool, before the sun comes up and starts sucking water from your body. Until then, moisture loss is mainly from breathing, and that's minimal. But later today, water's going to become critical. Push hard now, push hard and make the most of this time. You were the last one to start and that means you have to make up for the head start the rest of them have on you. Push hard.

I did. I moved as swiftly as I could on that black trail through the woods, and it wasn't long before I saw the beam of a flashlight bobbing along the trail in front of me. I caught up with and overtook the owner of the flashlight and then started overtaking and passing other flashlights. *Yeah, this is it. This is the way to make up for lost time.*

Within an hour and a half, I had caught up with and pulled ahead of at least half the group, but after that, I saw no one else. An hour later the darkness started to subside. Sunrise was a while off yet, but it would soon be light enough to see well. A gray smear showed through the trees in front of me. *Hmmm. That should be off to my right, because the trail is going north.* I reached for my compass. *Nah, probably just a temporary turn to the east before the trail swings north again.*

But the trail kept heading east and soon started to bend back to the south. *This isn't right,* I thought as the trail finally broke into a clearing and I had enough daylight to check my location. I dropped ruck and got out my map and compass.

Let's see, I should be about here on the map, about twenty kilometers up the trail. But the terrain looked nothing like it should.

I figured that at this distance from the start point, I should be on a long narrow ridge running due north. Instead, the trail was turning southeast and passing through a wide shallow valley that opened out to the east. The terrain wasn't distinct enough for me to do a resection, so instead I did a terrain analysis.

Wide shallow valley to the east, large rounded hill mass to the southwest, prominent ridge to the north, running from southwest to northeast. Nope . . . doesn't fit. But just for the sake of argument . . . if I had taken the old Uwharrie Trail branch instead of the new Uwharrie branch, I would be . . . exactly where I'm standing now! Holy cow! Good Lord almighty! How could I have been so stupid?

Of all the boneheaded rookie mistakes! I had saved all my potential screwups to let them loose in this one big, Fourth of July, Atomic Dumb-Bomb Attack! Man, oh man.

Now, let's see if I can unravel this knot. I'm twelve kilometers from the branch in the trail, which means that I should have been twelve kilometers up the new trail. That would put me about here, if I hadn't screwed up. That's a total of twenty-four kilometers if I backtrack, but just twenty kilometers if I cut cross-country to intercept the trail where I'd be right now if I hadn't fouled up. But I might as well intercept the trail where it crosses this hardtop road instead. That makes for a cross-country total of about twenty-seven kilometers, or sixteen miles, before I see the trail again. Well, I ain't gettin' there by standing around this clearing with my face hanging out. I've just turned the forty-miler into a fifty-five miler.

I saddled up and started moving.

So far throughout the course, I had taken a short break every hour. Sometimes the break was for ten minutes, sometimes for five, and occasionally for as short as three minutes. The length of the break was always predicated on how well I thought I was doing. Even a short break of a couple of minutes gives you a mental and physical lift that always leaves you stronger than when you sat down. But my breaks had to be severely limited now.

I pushed hard for two hours and then made a two-minute stop. Fortunately, I didn't have to stop for water; I could get at my canteens and drink on the move. It was critical that I drink plenty of water—at least a quart an hour—because if I became dehydrated, I'd eventually go down.

I stopped at a small spring bubbling from the base of a hill and filled my canteens. Then I dropped two iodine tablets into each canteen to purify the contents. My movement would thoroughly mix the tablets with the water, and it would be completely purified within thirty minutes.

On and on I pushed with a sense of urgency like never before. I adjusted my heading to hit the trail a few hundred meters before it intersected the road. I had trouble enough as it was without risking being caught on or too near a hard-top road by a cadre member. Shortly after noon I struck the trail and, a few minutes later, came out on the road. Major Odessa was waiting there and seemed not the least bit surprised by my sudden appearance.

"Seeing some of the countryside, are you?" he quipped. "I do wish you hadn't taken the wrong turn in the trail. It does so add to an already lengthy day."

"Yes sir, and I'm sure it hurts you more than it does me," I retorted as I crossed the road and reentered the trail.

"No, not at all," he replied. "I'm remarkably comfortable and pain free. But you, on the other hand . . . You know you can quit at any time. Wouldn't you like to quit now? There's no one here but you and me. It's an excellent time to quit. You know it's almost impossible to catch up. Why not quit now and save yourself an exercise in futility?"

He said the last sentence to my back as I walked past him and into the woods on the far side of the road.

"No thanks, Major," I said with a glance over my shoulder. He was beaming at me as if I had just won best dog in show. *Why did it have to be him? I'll bet he's been there for hours waiting for me, just for the pleasure of seeing my humiliation.*

Well, it wasn't much as far as humiliations go. I had never been lost, just befuddled for a while. But now that was behind me and I was back on track again. I pressed on with the strength born of desperation.

A couple of hours later, I finally caught up with

someone. It was Gorilla Man, and he was limping up the trail as if he had a flat tire.

"What happened to you?" I asked as I got close to him.

He looked up. "Once it got daylight, I took off my boots and put on my running shoes to wear between RVs. But I think I've got march fractures[2] now," he said between gritted teeth.

"Why not put your boots back on?" I said over my shoulder as I passed him.

"That's not a bad idea," he said wonderingly as he stopped and looked down at his feet. He sounded genuinely amazed by the advice.

Thank goodness for guys like that. Whenever you're feeling really stupid, they can show you that you're just an amateur in the field.

Within the next hour or so, I caught up with and overtook several other men. I had covered slightly more than thirty miles, but still had more than twenty to go. It was getting more and more difficult to do speed computations in my head. My hands were tingling from the rucksack straps cutting into my shoulders, pinching the nerves and arteries and restricting the blood flow to my arms.

I was bent forward against the weight of the rucksack. I felt as if I was dragging a train behind me, and my feet hurt all the way up to my knees. I don't mean they were just sore; I mean they felt as if I had been strapped to the rack and someone had beaten the balls of them with a bat. I tried to calculate the foot-pounds of energy my feet had absorbed so

---

[2] March fractures: the small bones of the feet can break from the pressure of carrying heavy loads for miles.

far that day, but had to give up the effort. I knew only that the accumulated tonnage of all those thousands of steps was immense. And it was only going to get worse.

There was an RV at the trail's end. My rucksack was weighed there, and I was sent up a gravel road through open farm country. After a while on the road, I started meeting guys coming back from the direction I was going. None of us had the spare energy even to nod to one another. We only exchanged pained glances of recognition.

The sun was about one fist above the horizon now, there was roughly an hour and a half of daylight left, and I still had a long way to go. I came to an RV at the end of a long sweeping bend in the road. I had been able to see it for ten minutes across the fields, and making my way there was absolute torture.

Carlos was the sitter. I plotted my next RV and reported back to him. "Change the batteries in your flashlight and then show me that it works," he instructed.

I did as he directed and then clipped the GI flashlight to the shoulder strap of my rucksack.

"You may continue to use roads and trails, but you are not restricted to them," he said after I had shown him the location of my next RV. I nodded, adjusted the straps of my rucksack, and was off again.

I continued to study my map as I made my way back down the road again. The gravel was especially painful to my feet. I walked in the ruts of the road, where the gravel had been smashed to the sides, but the stray stones there were even more painful.

It looked as though my best route was to follow this road for another kilometer, then move due west, cross-country and over a sharp ridge, to pick up a road paralleling this one in the next valley over. That road eventually intersected the one where the RV was located.

Darkness caught me before I reached the top of the ridge. The slope was covered in a tangle of mountain pine saplings and brush, but it was some relief to my legs to get off the road and climb. Once on top, I looked for the best way down. Far below, at the bottom of the slope, I could make out a light winking through the trees. *That must be the security light on the church down there.* My map showed a country church located along the road at the base of the ridge. As I made my way down the brush-tangled slope, that light was like a shore beacon to a sailor on a stormy sea. I zeroed in on it and ignored everything else.

When I was almost to the churchyard, I heard a voice call out, "Oh, Jesus! Somebody's finally there. Help me out of here! Help me! Come and get me."

It could be only one person.

I had been so focused on the light in the churchyard that I hadn't seen him. Parks was fifty meters to my left, tangled up in a two-acre patch of kudzu. He was thrashing and flailing like a man caught in quicksand going down for the last time.

"Over here, Parks. Take your time and walk straight to me. Stop fighting it and just walk slowly towards me. The more you fight it, the more tangled you're going to get."

"OK, man, OK," he mewled. "Just don't leave me. Wait until I get out."

Standing there and waiting for him to wade out of that field of kudzu was agony.

Don't get me wrong. I wasn't in agony over Parks' predicament. It just hurt worse to stand still than it did to

93

keep walking. As soon as he was almost to the edge, I continued lurching downhill to the church.

I was so exhausted now and my body was such a throbbing mass of pain that every little decision was a major undertaking. Parks caught up with me in the churchyard. I knew I had to go left on the road in front of the church, but telling my right from my left took a deliberate effort.

"Which way do we go?" Parks whined. "I don't think that's the right way," he said to my back as I turned and walked away. But I could hear the gravel crunching under his feet as he fell in behind and followed me down the road.

I slogged down the road into the growing darkness. I was done for. I no longer had any idea what time it was. I just knew it was some time after dark. My legs were solid aching masses, as heavy as concrete. My arms were completely numb. I could only maintain a hold on my grease gun by tucking its magazine well into the front waistband of my fatigue pants and pressing it there with my unfeeling clublike hands. My neck ached terribly from fighting the weight of the rucksack. My head had been thrust forward all day like a tortoise's head shoved out in front of its shell. My eyes pulsed with the pain of utter exhaustion. I was ready to quit.

That's it. The next RV is the last one. . . . No matter what, I'm not going any farther. I can't go any farther. But dang, the next RV just has to be the last one, doesn't it? Sure, it has to be. How far have I come? I don't know; I can't remember. I can't think anymore. All I can do is put one foot in front of the other. Left, right, left. One step and then another step. Just one more step. If I can just keep taking one more step, then I can keep going. Yep, I can keep going. I've come too far to quit now.

"Parks, shut up! Just shut up!"

Parks had been trailing along behind me, keeping up a continuous babble. "This is the wrong way. You're going the wrong way. We'll never get there this way. Is the next RV the finish? How much farther do you think it is? I can't make it anymore. I'm gonna quit. Don't leave me here! Don't leave me!"

I had to get away from him. His incoherent prattle was robbing me of what little energy I had left. From somewhere within the depths of my bowels, I summoned up a reserve of strength and increased my pace just as I hit the road junction. I turned to the right, in the direction of the RV, and left Parks standing at the intersection, mumbling to himself, whimpering that I was going the wrong way.

I stumbled down the road into the darkness and walked right into the RV. I almost bounced off the sitter's truck, then stood there swaying like a tree in the wind while Marvin gave me instructions. I could hear him clearly, but it seemed that it took a few seconds for me to understand what he had said. It was like listening underwater.

I plotted the next coordinates and reported back with my current location and the position of the next RV.

"From this point forward, the use of roads and trails is no longer authorized," said Marvin from the glow of his flashlight.

Oh no, that means I'll have to cross that river, and I don't have the strength to swim it. I left the RV on wooden legs, laboriously working out a plan in my head. *I'll have to find a steep bend in the river, build a poncho raft for my rucksack, and let the current push me to the other side. All I have to do is hang on. Then I'll change clothes . . . and leave my wet uniform behind, because I can't carry the additional weight of a waterlogged uniform. This is gonna be tough, but I can do it; I know I can.*

Just as I had taken a few steps away from the RV, someone stepped out of the darkness and stopped me with a hand on my chest. It was Major Odessa.

"Haney, you look like you're in pretty bad shape. Why don't you give it up before you hurt yourself?"

"Major, I'm not gonna quit, but I can't argue with you about it. Just let me go." I staggered as I tried to walk around him.

He kept his hand on my chest. "Hold it a second. Does your flashlight work? Does it have fresh batteries? Show me."

What's he screwing with me for? I don't have the energy for this. I fumbled with thick useless fingers, trying to find the sliding On button of the flashlight, and after much effort, I spilled a thin beam of light across the road.

"OK. That's good," he said as I leaned my weight forward to step away. "But you don't have to go any farther, Haney. You've finished. You have successfully completed Stress Phase and the forty-miler."

For a second I thought it was another trick, and I just stood there rocking back and forth as I tried to make out the meaning of what I had just heard. But as the words "successfully completed" finally came to rest in my consciousness, I saw the smile that had broken out on the major's previously stonelike face.

It was finally over.

Someone stepped up and pulled the rucksack from my back, and other hands guided me off the road, down a pathway into the woods. I was led to the side of a fire and lowered to the ground with my back propped against the bank of the path. Smiley, the medic, gently took my boots off, inspected my feet, and propped them up on my rucksack.

Someone else brought me a canteen cup of something from a kettle sitting on the fire: hot spiced wine. God, how delicious. I'd never tasted anything so perfect. Cadre members came over and shook my hand and said congratulations. Major Odessa came down and knelt beside me.

"You had me worried for a while this morning, Haney. I thought you had walked off the edge of the earth," he said with a smile.

"No sir, but it was darn near off the map sheet," I said, and took another sip of wine. It was a little peculiar: everyone was all smiles, everyone was concerned, everyone was helpful—where as previously, everything had been so impersonal. It felt good. It felt good to be finished. It felt good to be sitting there drinking. It all just felt good.

The cadre members drifted away and I was left resting against the bank, comfortably slurping hot wine. My legs were as stiff as rails. Same for my arms. But they would be all right the next day, and for now, it felt great just to be still and not have to move.

I looked at my watch: 2150 hours. *I finished about fifteen minutes ago, so let's round that off to 2130, I thought. I started this morning at 0330, so that means I walked for . . . eighteen hours.* I had covered more than fifty miles in eighteen hours and my feet sure knew it. But they had held up and served me well. I couldn't have asked any more of them. I wriggled my toes and flapped my feet back and forth. *Thanks, feet.*

I heard voices on the road. Parks was arguing with Marvin, but I couldn't make out what was being said. A few minutes later I heard Parks shouting and carrying on in an elated voice—the major must have told him he was finished.

So Parks had made that last turn in the right direction after all. A few minutes later, he was carried down and propped against the bank of the trail across the fire from me. He looked like hell, but he was almost delirious with joy at having completed the march.

He received the same postmarch care that I had enjoyed, and soon we were left alone to savor our victory in shared solitude. For once, his turbulent soul seemed at peace as we lounged there in silence, staring into the muttering fire and floating on our thoughts of the day.

Within an hour, three more fugitives increased the size of our happy campfire brotherhood. After they had been tended to and allowed to decompress a bit, we were guided or carried back up to the road, helped into the back of a truck, and stuffed down into sleeping bags for the trip back to Aberdeen Camp.

I never heard the sound of the engine cranking, and I knew nothing else until we were being helped out of the trucks back at camp. Two of the men could not be awakened and were carried into the barracks like sacks of grain and dropped on their bunks.

I hobbled in on terribly stiff sore legs and painful feet, fell on a cot, and immediately went back to sleep. The sun was up many hours before I was.

Before breakfast, we were herded outside in front of the

trucks, where Sergeant Major Shumate took the "after" picture, as he had promised.

There were 18 men in the photograph—18 out of the
original 163 who had started. But the Selection course still
wasn't over.

The commander's board was still to come.

CHAPTER**FIVE**

Our little band of walking wounded spent the rest of the morning limping around camp, cleaning and turning in our equipment. In the afternoon, we sat down in the classroom and filled out a peer report questionnaire. Since we didn't all know one another's names, we were identified by the numbered chairs we sat in. The questions were all subjective in nature:

Who do you think showed the most character? Who seemed the most competent? Who was the weakest? Who would you most want by your side in combat? Who would you least want by your side in combat? Who do you most trust? Who do you least trust? If you had to reject one man from this group, who would it be and why?

After completing the peer report, we were free for the remainder of the afternoon.

I was physically spent and sore in every part of my body. But as I reflected on what I had undergone, I felt a calm sense of satisfaction and contentment. I had not just survived an ordeal, because survival in a sense is passive. No, I had conquered. But conquered what? I had to think about that a while, and then I realized: myself.

I had undertaken a tremendously difficult challenge. Many men had tried and failed; only a few of us had stayed the course. And I didn't think a single man among us felt he did not merit the success he had earned. I was certainly sure I deserved to be there. It had been difficult, but I had done it solely on my own abilities. I was just glad that part was over. But the commander's board was still ahead. That, and an interview with the unit psychologist.

After supper that night, we found a schedule, listing the times of our meetings with the shrink posted on the bulletin board. We had already been reminded that this was still an individual effort, and we were forbidden to speak with any other candidate about the interview process.

I was the first one to report to the psychologist the following morning. I found him sitting in an easy chair tucked deep in a shadowed corner of an empty room. He didn't look up from the folder of papers he was studying. Then, with a languid wave of a pale hand, he indicated that I should take a seat on the lone steel chair in the center of the room.

I had expected a less interrogation-like setting, and the hair on the back of my neck suddenly started to rise. The only thing missing was a blinding white light shining in my eyes.

I sat down and waited.

The psychologist casually flipped back and forth through the papers in his lap and continued to ignore me. If his intent was to make me angry, it was working.

As I studied the man in his darkened corner, I saw that

he was a pudgy, effeminate-looking person with the longish hair of an academic. Behind his glasses his eyes appeared weak, as though they seldom saw the sun. A smug, superior air seemed to surround him, and when he finally spoke to me, it was off to one side, as though I was not worthy of his full attention. Without any preliminaries, or even an introduction, he launched straight into his program.

"Haney," he began. "I'm going to outline a hypothetical situation and I want you to tell me how you would handle it." His tone made it clear that he considered speaking to me distasteful.

"Your commander has selected you to take out a terrorist who has been located in San Francisco. Due to the need for secrecy and the delicacy of the task, neither the local authorities nor the FBI can be made aware of the mission. You must eliminate the terrorist and then make your way undetected out of the city and back to Fort Bragg. You can leave no trace of evidence that would lead back to this unit. Tell me how you would accomplish the task."

A simple tactical exercise. Not exactly what I expected in this interview, but oh well. Let me see how I would do this. I thought about the situation for a few minutes, and then, following the format of an operations order,[1] I outlined how I would go about accomplishing the mission.

The psychologist remained motionless while I talked, looking only at the papers he held on his lap. When I finished speaking, he maintained his silence for at least a full minute, still studying the papers that fascinated him so.

[1] The format of this order is 1. situation; 2. mission; 3. execution; 4. command and signal; 5. service and support.

Then, at last, he lifted his eyes to me for the first time and sneered at me from the shadows.

"You ignorant redneck. Have you never heard of the Posse Comitatus Act?[2] Don't you know it's against federal law for the military to be used for operations within the United States?"

Venom dripped from his tongue.

"And the mission wasn't to kill a terrorist at all, but to assassinate your commander's wife's lover. The reason he selected *you* for this mission was he knew you were such a lowlife simpleton that you would do what he wanted without question." He paused for a second before continuing.

"You stupid Southern Cracker. It's a good thing we have an army, so white trash like you can have a place to go rather than to the local chain gang, where you would doubtless be otherwise."

He watched me with hooded eyes before concluding. "What do you have to say for yourself now?"

Had I been my normal self, I could have laughed it all off and asked the man to try again. But in my still near-exhausted state, and without the full power of my faculties, I was hit by his words as if by a physical blow. No, that's not true. If it had been a physical assault, I would have known how to fight back. As it was, I was stunned and reeling. *How dare that desk jockey who's never seen a day of combat speak to me that way.* I felt belittled and at a complete loss as to what to do or say.

As I stared at my adversary in anger, I quickly realized

[2] Federal law states that the U.S. Military can't be used within the United States. Forget what you see in the movies. Soldiers don't fight on home turf without very, very special orders.

that it had been a setup. But I was enraged just the same. It was one thing to be made to look stupid, but he had insulted my background, and that was an assault on my honor. It was completely infuriating, and I was consumed with rage. The only thing saving the man from a severe beating was the fact that he was an officer.

Now it was obvious to me that the interview held one purpose: to mount a full-scale psychological assault and hit me where it would hurt. It had been masterfully executed. The man's objective had been to shake my self-confidence and see how I would act under pressure.

This is just like a prisoner of war interrogation, I thought. I'd learned a lot about interrogation in SERE school,[3] and I knew then that whatever I said would be wrong. I uttered one expletive and refused to talk anymore.

Every few minutes the guy would slide some nasty comment in my direction, but I kept my mouth shut. For the next ten minutes, I sat in my chair and stared at my interrogator, with the angry sound of my racing pulse pounding in my ears.

Eventually, he too must have realized that this wasn't going any further and that he had all he was going to get from me. He waved the pudgy white fingers of one hand in my general direction and, shifting his gaze back to his papers once again said, "We're finished here. Why don't you go away?"

---

[3] All members of the special operation forces must attend SERE training (survival, evasion, resistance, and escape) to prepare them for the possibility of being captured, interrogated, and possibly tortured by a hostile adversary. It's no fun, but it helps.

With pleasure.

I felt beat-up, violated, and helpless to do anything about it. By the time all of us had undergone our interviews with that man, I found out I wasn't alone in my reaction. In fact, he had managed to destroy so completely the sense of trust necessary in his relationship with the unit that none of us would ever speak to him again. Subsequent unit psychologists were aghast that we had been subjected to such stupid treatment from someone we'd be expected to respect enough to learn from in the future. The man soon left the army to pursue "other opportunities."

All the interviews were finished by late that evening, and since a new class of candidates would be arriving the next day to start Selection, we were sent back to the main post at Fort Bragg to await our appearance before the commander's board. In the meantime we would be staying at Moon Hall, where we had originally signed in.

Moon Hall is a military hotel complex, and by any standards, it's quite a facility. There are also a great NCO Club annex in one of the buildings and a mess hall that would knock your socks off.

Every Friday the mess was open all afternoon—from lunch through supper—continuously offering up a succession of steamship rounds for sacrifice. Breakfast every day was a thing of beauty, and brunch on Saturdays and Sundays was out of this world.

The mess sergeant (or dining facility manager, as he was called in official army newspeak) was a national award–winning chef who was hired for an astronomical salary by a New York hotel when he retired from the military. And considering the acclaim of everyone who ever ate in his mess, he deserved every cent of that salary.

We loafed around Fort Bragg for several days. The commander's board would not convene for a while, and until then, we were to relax and recuperate. We had an informal formation in the lobby every morning at 1000 and then were released to our own control.

I was glad for the downtime. It turned out that I had gotten a march fracture in my left foot during the forty-miler. I thought I knew when it had happened, but by that point in the march, my feet had been so numb that the pain hadn't been able to register. After a few days' rest, I felt fine.

Doc Smiley met us in the lobby one morning and told us that the board would convene the next day. We were to report in fatigue uniform to Aberdeen Camp the next morning at 0800.

So the last hurdle was at hand. The next day I would learn my fate: acceptance or rejection. I would not even contemplate being turned away. But if that happened, I'd face it in its own time. The next day I would also finally meet the commander of the unit, Colonel Charlie (not Charles) Beckwith. I knew almost nothing about the man; I'd never heard of him prior to my arrival at Selection. But most of the SF soldiers knew of him, and a few had served near him, if not with him, in Vietnam and other locations around the world.

The reports on Colonel Beckwith were a mixed lot. Some said he was a hell of a commander; others said he was an egomaniac with a reputation for getting his troops killed. But the reports made little difference to me.

Commanders came and commanders went. If a unit had decent troops, it would survive. With a good commander, a good unit could prosper; with a bad one, a good unit could hold its own. And after what I'd seen during Selection, I could tell by the mere handful of men in the unit so far that this was going to be one heck of an outfit.

I suspected that if Beckwith was crazy, it was a good kind of crazy. He was, and it was, but all that in good time.

My board appearance was scheduled for 1500 hours. We were severely cautioned against speaking to one another about anything that was said or done within the board.

The morning and afternoon dragged by. I'm a patient man, but on that day, I could barely contain myself. I'd sit inside the waiting room for a while and then go outside to talk nervously with the other "waiters." Men were called and they disappeared inside. The first three men interviewed came out of the room ashen-faced and refused to look at us as they reported to the orderly room for orders to return to their home units.

Rejected. Not accepted for assignment. Cold, hard, devastating words. My guts chilled and settled into a hard freeze as I watched those men, one by lonely one, walk away. Just like the dead and wounded stretched out after a firefight, they had my sympathy, but I was glad I wasn't among them.

I was also glad they left camp immediately and didn't say any awkward farewells. They were social lepers, and I didn't want to risk catching the infection they carried. I wasn't proud of feeling that way, but I had to admit that it was true.

Finally, two men in a row came out of that room so elated that they looked as if they would explode. We could tell they wanted to jump up and down or dance out of the sheer pleasure of winning. Smiley led each of them away before they could say anything to those of us still waiting in limbo.

Then it was my turn.

OK, Eric, this is it. Compose yourself, keep your wits about you, and be ready for anything. Smiley told me to walk to the front of the room, halt in front of the chair, and report to the commander—just as for any other board appearance. I gave my uniform a quick check, brought myself to the position of attention, picked up a thousand-yard stare, took a deep breath, and marched through the door into the lion's den.

I halted in front of the chair, with just enough space in front of me that when I turned about I would be able to sit straight down without having to look for the chair or back up to take my seat. I executed a parade ground about-face, whipped up a quivering salute, waited two counts, and growled out in my best platoon sergeant voice, "Sir! Sergeant Haney reports to the commander!"

It was my first view of Colonel Beckwith. I was looking at a point in space just above his head, but I could still clearly see him—a big man sprawled across the folding chair directly in front of me.

His face was fierce, almost belligerent. I learned later that that was the expression he used for most occasions. He had a shock of slate gray hair, a wide forehead, and piercing eyes set deep in his face, with dark circles underneath. His cheekbones were high, but not prominent. His nose was hawklike, but not large. His jawline looked as if it had been shaped by an axe. His lower lip was pushed out slightly, giving him an insolent air. His chest and shoulders were deep and wide, and his belly was expansive. All in all, he looked just like what he was—a warrior chieftain surrounded by his lieutenants.

He let me hold my position while he looked me up and down several times; then he finally returned my salute and told me to sit down. The attack commenced.

"Haney, I understand you don't like officers," were the first words he hurled at me, dredged up from somewhere deep within his chest.

I had told myself before this started that I would be brutally honest and not tap-dance around any question. They were going to get Staff Sergeant Eric Haney, raw and in person. I was going to give them the whole log, with the bark still on it, no matter what the consequences.

"That's correct, sir." I fastened my eyes on his as I spoke. "I despise most of the officers I've ever met."

He came unglued. His face swelled and turned red, and the veins in his neck bulged out. But I was determined to take no crap.

"Haney, that's mutiny!" he shouted at me. "What in flaming Hades is wrong with you? How could you make a statement like that?"

"Sir, most of the officers I've met spend the majority of their time scheming for career progression and looking for ways to stab each other in the back. The only good thing about that is they usually leave the NCOs and the soldiers alone to get on with unit business—at least until they want to put on some kind of dog and pony show to impress someone with how great they are."

From the corner of my eye, I could see Sergeant Major "Country" Grimes trying to suppress a grin. *Ah, just maybe I have one ally in the room.*

Beckwith ranted and raved until eventually his anger lost steam. He looked at me as if I was a biological specimen. Then he leaned back in his chair, swelled out his chest, and asked in an arrogant voice, "Well then, Sergeant Smart-Mouth, what did you think of Stress Phase?"

"Sir, I kept waiting for the stress to start."

"You what?" He leapt from his chair. "You kept waiting for the stress to start? What in heaven's name do you mean by that? Are you out of your mind?" His face was so swollen with rage, I thought he might have a stroke. He stood there gasping for air and gaping at me.

"Sir, I ate four meals a day and slept at least eight hours every night. No one was shooting at me. I never stepped on a land mine. The weather was good. I never got frostbite or had heat exhaustion. I was responsible for myself and no one else. Yep, it was hard. In some ways, the hardest thing I've ever done. But, sir, there are more difficult things in life than Selection."

He huffed and puffed about that until he thought up something else to slap me with. And that was the way it went.

We took turns yelling at each other. He told me the Rangers were a bunch of pansies, and I told him he was full of mud. He told me I was just a parade ground soldier, and I countered that he obviously hadn't read my record, because I'd never served a day in anything but combat units.

Beckwith would rant until he literally ran out of breath, and then someone else in the room would come at me with something different. I was getting it from all sides, like a bear with its back to a cliff while a pack of hounds lunged in and snapped at its flanks. It got so intense I thought I was going to have to fight.

At one point, Beckwith said he'd had enough of my disrespect and was just going to have Sergeant Russell here kick my butt, indicating a big hard-looking man seated on the front row.

I stared at Russell, turned back to look the colonel straight in the face, and told him that was one order he'd better not give unless he wanted to see me thrash his man. I looked back at Russell, who held my gaze and smiled slightly. I got my feet under me, ready to jump if I had to. If Beckwith ordered Russell at me, I would kick him in the face and take him out of the fight before he could get out of his chair. I'd only get one chance.

We took a breather then. It was as if the bell had rung and the colonel and I fell back in our chairs, panting like two boxers between rounds. I'd been taking some big punches, but I felt that I had thrown a few good ones of my own. Then Sergeant Major Grimes broke the heavy quiet.

"Haney," he said in his Pennsylvania mountain twang, "the peer reports of the other men indicated they don't think very highly of you. Said they thought you were a pretty poor example of a soldier." His voice was calm and measured, and he watched me intently, one eye squinted as if he was inspecting a rifle barrel.

I thought for a few seconds about what he had said. Then I answered. "Sergeant Major, that's crap and you know it. You're just trying to rattle my cage. I'm the best soldier those men have ever met in their military lives."

Grimes stifled another grin.

Someone on the other side of the room—someone who just *had* to be an officer—wagged his finger at me and accused me of being evasive. Said I'd refused to answer all the questions in my psychological battery.

I asked him what he was talking about, and he held up a sheet of paper and read aloud, " 'I love my mother, but . . . '

"Why didn't you complete the sentence?" he yelled at me, shaking the rolled sheet of paper in the air.

"There's nothing to complete," I said. "I love my mother, no buts about it. Don't try to put your feelings about your own mother off on me."

"Colonel, I've had enough," he said, turning to look at Colonel Beckwith. "This man can't give a straight answer to the simplest question. He's been nothing but insolent and disrespectful since he walked in the door. I, for one, have seen and heard enough."

The colonel nodded. Looking at me, he said, "Get out and wait till I call for you." He dismissed me with a jerk of his thumb toward the door.

I stood and saluted. He waved what could only vaguely be called a salute in my general direction as I marched for the door and exercised the utmost of my self-control to keep from slamming it behind me. I stalked to the far end of the hall and paced back and forth in a four-foot square. I was wound up more tightly than a two-dollar watch.

One of my Selection mates, Jimmy Johnson, could stand it no longer and came down to talk to me. I cut him off with a raised hand before he could open his mouth and draw breath.

"Jimmy, don't ask me anything. You know I can't answer,

and you'll put us both in a tight spot if you don't just go away. Now, leave me alone." With that I turned my back on him and paced in the opposite direction.

The men at the other end of the hall stared at me as if I had anthrax.

A few minutes later, Smiley came out of the conference room and beckoned me to go with him into another room. It was the medical station.

"Read the chart on the wall," he said. "All lines, top to bottom."

"With my glasses or without?"

"With."

I read them and then asked, "What's this all about?"

"The colonel wants to know how well you can see. Very few men who wear glasses have made it through Stress Phase. Now come with me. He wants you back inside. Just take your seat; you don't have to report again."

I went back to my chair and stared at Colonel Beckwith. He looked at Smiley and asked, "Well?"

Smiley nodded. "Colonel, his vision is fine with his glasses."

The colonel turned his eyes to me. His gaze was still fierce, but the belligerence was gone. "Well, Haney," he said with just the slightest lilt of humor in his voice, "you've got a little bit of a temper on you, once you get roused, don't you?"

"Yes sir, I'm afraid I do."

"And you've got a smart mouth to go along with it, don't you?"

"Yes sir, I have one of those, too."

"And you're kind of prone to shooting from the hip, sort of rapid-fire-like, when somebody pokes at you, aren't you?"

"Yes sir, I'd say that's also true."

He pushed out his lower lip and paused in reflection for a few seconds before continuing. "Well, son, so am I, and it ain't necessarily bad all the time. The trick is knowing when it'll work and when it won't. But I like your style and I want you with us."

He stood as he said the last sentence and extended a bear paw of a hand in my direction. I looked at his hand, looked at his face, and smiled. I grabbed his outstretched hand, gave it a good shake, and felt the power of his grip. The other men in the room crowded around and offered their congratulations.

"Welcome aboard," they said. "Good to have you with us."

Grimes grinned at me. "Just rattling your cage, eh?"

"Yes, Sergeant Major. That's what you were doing, wasn't it?"

"Yeah, it was, and I thought I'd gotten to you for a second there."

"You came mighty close, Sergeant Major, you sure did."

And that was it. I had made it. I was a member of the newest, most elite unit in the national inventory.

When the board completed its business, there were twelve new members of First Special Forces Operational Detachment–Delta. Of the original 163 men who started Selection, 18 had passed Stress Phase and 12 had survived the commander's board. Four men had been rejected outright, and two others were told they could try again at a future date. Both did, and both were eventually selected.

The success rate for this Selection course was slightly above 7 percent. It would turn out to be the highest in Delta Force history.

I returned to Hunter Army Airfield to out-process and move my family to Fort Bragg. Jim Bush and I were the first men from the Ranger battalion to make it into the mysterious new unit. And the fact that we couldn't say anything about it just added to our celebrity.

I packed up, said my farewells, and headed out for a new phase of life. I had no idea what I was in for. When I look back at the young man I was then, I can only shake my head in wonder at the good fortune he carried with him to that new assignment.

Life would be difficult most of the time, and dangerous almost all the time. And every once in a while, it would be utterly deadly.

PART**TWO**

Preparing the Force:
The Training of a
Delta Force Operator

CHAPTER**SIX**

The Selection course immediately following mine produced eleven more successful candidates. Together, we all signed in to Delta Force in November and December of 1978.

With our arrival, the number of operator candidates in the unit was doubled. Now, in addition to the original administrative staff Colonel Beckwith had chosen, there would be enough people to run Selection, train the men already in the unit, and conduct a formal training course for those of us who had just arrived. Critical mass had been reached, though just barely. We were still short of the numbers needed to bring the unit to operational strength. That would take at least one more year.

I reported for assignment to the Fort Bragg stockade, our home and headquarters for the next eight years. The unit needed a large secure facility, and this was just about a perfect fit for us at the time.

The army was changing its method of handling prisoners. Soldiers convicted by court-martial and sentenced to incarceration were no longer being held in local installation facilities, but instead would all be remanded to Fort Leaven-worth. At Fort Bragg, that left a big, beautiful, brand-new high-security facility (translation: jail) almost empty. Colonel Beckwith snapped it up.

All we had to do to convert it to our use was cut the bunks loose from the floors in the dormitory bays and put up a few walls for class and conference rooms. We screened the chain-link fence surrounding the compound to restrict the view from outside, and last but not least, we planted rose gardens around the building's entrance. A nice touch.

The civilian guards who controlled access at the front gate and patrolled the grounds of the compound were all re-tired Special Forces sergeant majors, a hard, dedicated, seri-ous group of men.

Chief Guard Hugh Gordon was one of my favorites. Gordon had been one of the very first members of Special Forces back in the early 1950s. During World War II he had parachuted into Normandy with the Eighty-second Air-borne Division on his nineteenth birthday. He was repre-sentative of the men who provided our exterior security, and you can believe me when I tell you that security was never breached. Not even by us.

One night, after a training exercise, Doc Smiley decided to take a shortcut to the building and climbed the back fence rather than walking all the way around to the front gate. The next day, he told us that he had been straddling the top of the fence when he'd heard a pump shotgun rack a shell into the chamber and a calm voice announce, "Just drop your tail to the ground on this side of the fence."

All the way to the ground, Smiley kept saying, "Don't

Basic training platoon, 1970. I'm in the top row, sixth from the right—seventeen years old.

AFZP-IB-CSM   27 November 1978

SUBJECT: Letter of Appreciation

Staff Sergeant Eric Lamar Haney
254-▮▮▮▮▮
Company C, 1st Battalion (Ranger), 75th Infantry
Hunter Army Airfield, Georgia 31409

1. On your departure from the 1st Ranger Battalion, I would like to express
my appreciation for your manner of performance and loyal support.

2. Your vast knowledge of Infantry weapons, tactics and your exceptional
abilities as an instructor contributed greatly to the outstanding performance
of your platoon in all phases of training. Your close supervision, attention
to detail and devoted assistance to others in the unit was clearly demonstrated
at all times. You always insured your squad and team leaders warekept well
informed and ready to accomplish any mission assigned to you or in support
of the company and Battalion. Your initiative, resourcefulness, and untiring
efforts to achieve perfection in all phases of your duties resulted in increased
morale and esprit de corps in your platoon.

3. Your military bearing, dedication, physical fitness and professionalism
make you an asset to any organization. You could always be counted upon in any
situation to give a hundred and ten percent and make the decisions necessary to
excell in every area. I am certain you will continue to excell in all your
endeavors and move on to the top of the Noncommissioned Officers Corp. Your
high standards of appearance, military courtesy, cheerful and cooperative
approach to all problems and task encountered have drawn many favorable comments
from superiors and subordinates alike.

4. You can take great pride in the remarkable performance of duty rendered
to this Battalion. I charge you to continue to lead the way. Your actions
reflect great credit upon yourself, the 1st Ranger Battalion and the US Army.

                    "RANGERS LEAD THE WAY"

                            Glen E. Morrell
                            GLEN E. MORRELL
                            CSM, IN
                            Command Sergeant Major

Letter from Command Sergeant Major Glen Morrell
on my departure from First Ranger Battalion.

My "after" photo from Selection, the morning after the Forty Miler. Another six men in the photo were later cut by the commander's board. I'm in the second row, first on the left.

B Squadron, early winter, 1982. I'm in the center row, fifth from the right.

Remnants of B Squadron at Grenada.

Embassy and local credentials used in
Beirut, Haiti, and Honduras.

ENLISTED EVALUATION REPORT
(AR 623-205)

Proponent agency for this form is the US Army Military Personnel Center.

PART I. ADMINISTRATIVE DATA

A. LAST NAME – FIRST NAME – MIDDLE INITIAL	B. SSN	C. RANK (ABBR)	D. DATE OF RANK
HANEY, ERIC L.	254-	MSG	830313

E. PRIMARY MOSC	F. SECONDARY MOSC	G. UNIT, ORGANIZATION, STATION, ZIP CODE/APO, MACOM
11B5V	19Z5C	1st Special Forces Operational Detachment-DELTA (Airborne) Fort Bragg, North Carolina 28307-5000 (DA)

H. CODE/TYPE OF REPORT	I. PERIOD OF REPORT				J. RATED MONTHS	K. NONRATED MONTHS	L. NONRATED CODES
3 Change of Rater	FROM YEAR 85	MONTH 04	THRU YEAR 85	MONTH 11	8	NONE	NA

PART II. DUTY DESCRIPTION

A. PRINCIPAL DUTY TITLE: Senior Instructor/Training   B. DUTY MOSC: 11B5P

C. DESCRIPTION OF DUTIES: Primarily serves as a Senior Instructor/Trainer in the six month Operator Training Course. The course, conducted semi-annually, is designed to prepare operator designates for service in the unit's operational Sabre Squadrons. Serves as a principle in planning, preparing, conducting, and evaluating numerous special operations training programs. Performs LNO functions with DOD and other government agencies. Provides senior NCO leadership, management, and supervision in conducting special operations training.

PART III. EVALUATION OF PROFESSIONALISM AND PERFORMANCE

RATER	INDORSER	A. PROFESSIONAL COMPETENCE	SCORING SCALE	RATER	INDORSER	B. PROFESSIONAL STANDARDS
5	5	1. Demonstrates initiative.	(High)	5	5	1. Integrity.
5	5	2. Adapts to changes.		5	5	2. Loyalty.
5	5	3. Seeks self-improvement.	5	5	5	3. Moral courage.
5	5	4. Performs under pressure.	4	5	5	4. Self-discipline.
5	5	5. Attains results.	3	5	5	5. Military appearance.
5	5	6. Displays sound judgment.		5	5	6. Earns respect.
5	5	7. Communicates effectively.	2	5	5	7. Supports EO/EEO.
5	5	8. Develops subordinates.	1	35	35	SUBTOTALS
5	5	9. Demonstrates technical skills.				
5	5	10. Physical fitness.	0			(Add the Rater's SUBTOTALS (A&B) and enter sum in the appropriate box in PART VI, SCORE SUMMARY. Do the same for Indorser.)
50	50	SUBTOTALS	(Low)			

C. DEMONSTRATED PERFORMANCE OF PRESENT DUTY   8512/PASS   74/165   YES

1. Rater's Evaluation: During this period, MSG Haney has played a very important role in elevating the proficiency of newly assigned personnel to 1st SFOD-D's Operator Training course as well as the combat readiness of this unit. On a daily basis he proves himself to be highly skilled in all aspects of sensitive, low-visibility operations. He is always ready to deploy independently or as a team member to accomplish any mission, real world or training at a moments notice. His ability to communicate with the highest government officials on matters important to national security places him in high regard by everyone he comes in contact with. MSG Haney also plays a very important role in recruiting new personnel into this unit. His credibility within the elite units such as the rangers has brought many outstanding young NCO's to 1st SFOD-D. He is constantly striving to improve his education during off duty time.

2. Indorser's Evaluation: MSG Haney is an outstanding NCO and Operator. He was chosen as a senior instructor because of his leadership, ability to communicate, and technical skills as an Operator. He is tough, quiet, and exceptionally talented in all aspects of low-visibility operations. He is extremely competent in all means of low-visibility infiltration. His ability in an austere field environment is without equal. In his present capacity he is frequently chosen to represent this unit to other government agencies, private organizations, and to foreign governments. He is equally comfortable with superiors and subordinates alike. The new Operators readily respond to his positive, firm leadership. He is a strong, dynamic factor in the growth and development of this unit. I want to continue to serve with this fine NCO.

DA FORM OCT 81 **2166-6**   REPLACES DA FORM 2166-5A, OCT 79, WHICH IS OBSOLETE.

My 1985 annual efficiency report as a senior instructor for OTC.

A critical commando task—baking bread.

shoot, Huck. It's me, Smiley." Mr. Huckaby then walked him to the front gate and logged him in. When he turned to walk away, Huckaby said he'd known who it was all along—otherwise he would have shot him off the top of the fence. None of us tried hopping the fence after that incident. Huck died at his post about ten years later, sitting on the ground, his back against the fence and his shotgun across his lap. He had suffered a heart attack while patrolling the perimeter. God bless old veterans.

Our band of new members received the designation "OTC-3," which stood for Operators Training Course Number Three. We were the third group of men into the unit. The first had been Colonel Beckwith and his administrators. The second had come from the first two Selection courses, and our group had come from the following two Selection courses.

We settled on the name "operator" to designate an operational member of the unit (as opposed to a member of the administrative and support staff) due to some legal and political considerations. We couldn't use "operative" because that name had certain espionage connotations from the CIA. The term "agent" had some legal issues.

An agent carries a legal commission to perform certain duties, and a governmental authority empowered by a state or federal constitution issues that commission. In our case, we would perform our duties under the authority of the federal government as administered by the Department of Defense and the Department of the Army.

But in the military, only officers carry legal commissions from the president and are confirmed by Congress. Sergeants, who are noncommissioned officers, are authorized to perform their duties by virtue of appointment by the secretary of the army. Sergeants, therefore, cannot be agents of the government. And since almost every operational member of Delta Force was a sergeant, we needed to choose a different name for ourselves. Hence, operator.

Delta Force was loosely patterned on the organizational structure of the British 22 Special Air Service Regiment. The forerunner of the SAS had inflicted damage greatly out of proportion to its size during World War II, using small teams of well-trained, independent-minded men to wreak havoc deep behind enemy lines.

The smallest Delta unit was the four-man team. Four or five teams, along with a small headquarters element, made up a troop. Two troops—an assault troop and a sniper troop—formed a squadron. Each squadron had a small command element. When OTC-3 finished its training, it formed two squadrons: A Squadron and B Squadron. These were known as the saber squadrons.

The selection and training detachment, like the saber squadrons, was composed of operators. We also had a signal squadron, which provided direct communication support for the unit, and the normal contingent of administrative, intelligence, operational planning, and support elements.

At the top of the pyramid were the commander, the deputy commander, the executive officer, the command sergeant major, and members of the commander's staff, such as the unit surgeon and psychologist.

The very best people in the army within their respective disciplines filled Delta Force's nonoperational functions. We operators always knew that we were backed up and supported by the absolute masters of any profession, no matter what their specialties—parachute riggers, administrative and finance clerks, cooks, supply personnel, communications specialists, and gunsmiths. You name the job, Delta folks were the best at it.

Delta's original plan called for three operational squadrons, but it would take more than ten years to realize that goal. Even during the first year, we had a difficult time keeping our numbers steady because injuries and pressure took such a heavy toll. Further growth proved so slow and painful that the third Delta squadron would not be formed until 1990, prior to Operation Desert Storm. Just a few short years later, in October 1993, C Squadron would be decimated in a horrific fight in Somalia, and the unit would have to rebuild itself. But in the fall of 1978, that was all in the distant future. For now we had other tasks at hand.

Our training program was scheduled to start the first week of January 1979, immediately after the holiday season. Until then, we busied ourselves with labor and construction projects such as readying the compound, finishing the newly constructed shooting house, and building our new range complex. While we were preparing the facilities, our instructors were preparing to lead us through the training program that would mold us into counterterrorist operators.

Colonel Beckwith had personally selected the team of four men who would be our lead instructors. Earlier in the summer, they had been trained in counterterrorist tactics and techniques by a visiting team of training experts from the SAS. In addition, we would receive assistance from visiting instructors and lecturers from other government agencies such as the FBI Academy; the CIA; the State Department; the Federal Aviation Administration; the Bureau of Alcohol, Tobacco, and Firearms; the Defense Nuclear Agency; the Department of Energy; and the United States Marshals Service.

We would also have the benefit of guest speakers and experts on terrorism from the academic world. From the very beginning, Delta's training was planned as the most extensive and in-depth program of instruction ever created, dedicated solely to producing a counterterrorist fighter such as the world had never known. And it only got better with time and experience. The idea of constant, ever-evolving training was a very different approach to the task, one never taken by any organization before. And everything in our lives would be different from then on.

Upon assignment to Delta Force, we ceased to exist in the regular army. Delta Force was (and is) a *secret* organization. Then, as now, it had no official existence on the rolls of army units, and neither did its members. We simply disappeared from the system. Our records were pulled and, from then on, were managed within a secret system known as the Department of the Army Security Roster (DASR).

We had a cover organization on Fort Bragg that we used as our "official" unit. That organization has an official address, a commander and a first sergeant, and someone to answer phones and provide a backstop. It provides a first level of "cover for status" and is useful for those everyday matters of life such as listing your employer or unit of assignment on credit applications, or telling your neighbors where you work. Forget trying to find it: the name of the unit and its phone numbers change every few years so as not to get worn out from overuse.

We disappeared from the military in other ways also. We lived on civilian clothing status and almost never wore a uniform. A relaxed grooming policy allowed us to grow longer hair and beards, making it easier to blend in when operating undercover. And after all, if we needed to look military, it was much easier to get a haircut quickly than it was to reverse the process.

As Mao Tse-tung said, "The guerilla swims in the sea of the people." And in Delta Force, we operated like guerillas. Or terrorists. Because the reality was that to become experts at counterterrorism, we first had to become expert terrorists.

We became completely insular in our relationships with outsiders. We didn't talk with anyone outside the unit about what we did—not even our families. Within the unit, we operated strictly on a need-to-know basis. If a teammate or friend disappeared for a while, we never asked where he had been or what he'd been doing when he returned. If he had been on a new type of mission we needed to know about, we were told of it in a briefing session for all the operators.

So in very short order, operational security (OPSEC) became our religion, and we naturally tended to restrict our dealings with outsiders. It became such habit that, even today, when someone asks me what I do for a living or where I'm from, my first reaction is to give an evasive answer.

Just so you know: there is nothing in this book that violates OPSEC. What you're reading is just the tip of the iceberg.

* * *

During that formative period, Delta's formal operator training course (OTC) was six months long. Later years saw the addition of an accelerated military free-fall parachuting course, but the principal areas of instruction and the length of the course have remained constant over time.

Our course would last from January to the end of June 1979. During that time, we would master the skills we needed to accomplish our mission. We would also develop new tactics and techniques for use within the organization.

Shooting is both a science and an art. The science of shooting is principally concerned with exterior ballistics:[1] what a projectile does in flight, how fast it initially takes off, how well it retains energy, what its flight path is in relation to the sight path, how it is affected by atmospheric conditions, what it does upon impact, and how it delivers its energy to a target.

A few other scientific matters concern the mechanics of the equipment—the consistency of powder loads and bullet weights and shapes, the accuracy of a barrel, and a gun's inherent tightness or sloppiness.

But the art of shooting is purely human. That comes into the picture when we hold a gun with these pulsing, trembling, quivering, and shaking bodies of ours. We must calculate all sorts of variables and try to make a round go off at just the precise instant that will cause a bullet to impact a tiny spot exactly where it was intended to go. At a distance, even the thump of your heartbeat can throw a shot off. (That's the reason Delta Force operators are trained to shoot

---

[1] Ballistics: the science or study of the motion of projectiles. It is a science in which geometry and mathematics become life or death.

between heartbeats.) Even if you're very good at shooting, you're never quite satisfied. And when you first start out, it can be a humbling exercise.

But the mastery of this skill is ground zero for the Delta Force operator. Without it, he would be some other type of being. Because when it gets right down to it, a Delta operator is an extremely skilled killer. He is like the wolf that becomes a shepherd. He will guard the flock, but—make no mistake about it—he remains a deadly predator.

Shooting is divided into two categories—short-gun shooting and long-gun shooting—and so are operators. Assault team members are known as short gunners, and sniper/observers are called long gunners.

Everyone in OTC is trained on the long gun, as a sniper/observer, because long-range shooting plays an important role in Delta's work. Men chosen for sniper troops are given specific—and exhaustive—training following their assignments.

Instead of training with a fancy sniper rifle, we used the army's standard M14, the predecessor of the M16. The M14 is the lineal descendent of the M1 Garand of World War II fame.

The M14 is heavier than the M16, fires a much larger round, and has greater range and power. Dressed up and accurized (fine-tuned for accuracy), it is an excellent gun for target match shooting. The army used it, modified and mounted with a ranging telescope, as a sniper rifle for years. Delta snipers still use it for certain tasks, but for the purposes of training, we used it in its plain-Jane form. There's no point in learning to drive a Porsche until you've mastered a Ford.

We spent our first three weeks of the course on the rifle range. It was a good, stress-free way to get to know one another. It gave us a chance to change some initial impressions we had of the other men in the course.

There had been two guys in Selection whom I had disliked on sight, and it had turned out that the feeling was mutual. Even though we probably never spoke to one another during Selection, my dislike for them continued to build in the weeks before we started OTC.

One guy was a stocky Californian from the Fifth Special Forces Group at Fort Bragg. The other was a dark, muscular guy from the infantry brigade in Alaska. I don't know why I disliked them so much in Selection, but by the time we got to OTC, I was prepared to despise them. And they were equally prepared to return the favor.

It turned out that the Californian, Jerry Knox, was a fireball of a man. He had a sly sense of humor and more intensity of character than almost any man I'd ever known. The muscle man, J. T. Robards, was utterly courageous—one of the most courageous men I'd ever met.

J.T. hated parachuting. He said he was terrified of it. I was jump-mastering one day, and as we were chuting up, J.T. kept up a running commentary about how much he hated jumping and how much it scared him. Checking his equipment prior to boarding, I asked him in exasperation, "If you hate it so much, J.T., why've you stayed in airborne units for the last fifteen years? It's voluntary, you know."

He looked at me in surprise and said, "I just like being with the kind of guys who *like* to do it."

During OTC, we developed profound respect for each

other and formed lifelong friendships. And that extended to every member as we jelled into a cohesive unit. It was the best group of men I've ever been associated with in my life.

We had our differences now and again. That's only natural of any tight-knit clan—all the more so when it's a clan populated by tough-minded men. But we always worked out our problems, even if the working out got a little heated.

There was one ironclad rule in Delta: never lay an angry hand on a brother operator. That was unforgivable and would result in immediate dismissal. It happened only once during my eight years in the organization, and I don't believe it has ever happened since.

So those first few weeks on the rifle range were valuable for a number of reasons. We got to know the character of our comrades and we laid a common foundation on which to build core skills. Potential snipers were identified, chosen both for their natural talent and for their inclination to serve in that capacity. In those early days, we didn't have the luxury of taking years to develop sniper troops.

The clock was already ticking, faster than we realized.

CHAPTER**SEVEN**

The principal tools of the Delta Force assault team member are pistols and submachine guns. Initially, both of our short guns fired the same round: .45-caliber automatic pistol.

Our submachine gun was the old World War II–era M3 grease gun we'd used in Selection. We used that model instead of a more modern design because Colonel Beckwith had snagged a warehouse full of them free from the CIA, and Charlie never could pass up a good deal. One of our guys complained about having to take so many of them, but Beckwith retorted, "You ain't got to feed 'em, and you don't have to shovel crap out from under 'em, so what are you complaining about?"

With practice, the grease gun is an easy weapon to use. Even given its poor sights and limited range, its .45-caliber round gives it some pretty impressive power. Within a year, we adopted the German-made Heckler & Koch model MP5 to replace it, but we kept a few grease guns around to use as silenced weapons. It was unsurpassed in that mode. The round is subsonic, so it doesn't give off a crack as it passes through the air, but it's heavy enough to retain a lot of energy and killing power.

Our pistol was an accurized version of Colt's M1911A1, the old army standby. This .45-caliber pistol is a big hard-hitting weapon, inherently accurate but difficult to master. Each operator has two, and they are the weapons he uses more than anything else for close-in work.

Pistols are trade-offs. You trade power, range, and accuracy for portability and concealability. With the .45, we kept the power we wanted, and constant intensive training gave us the range and accuracy.

Our primary pistol-shooting method was called instinctive fire, and it is considered a fundamental skill for deadly combat at close range. Most pistol shooting is based on the methods used in target shooting, such as staring at the front sight while shooting. But a close-range gunfight is a world away from target shooting, and then some.

Combat shooting is more akin to wing shooting—shooting birds on the wing—and you can only do it by watching the target and giving it your full concentration. Rather than smoothly squeezing the trigger until the gun goes off, you have to slap the trigger at just the right instant to hit the target. And before you can shoot a target, you must identify it. You have to determine *who the terrorist is*. You have to separate the deadly threat from the innocent bystander. And to do that effectively, you have to look at *people* instead of your *sights*. If your training has taught you to look at your sights, and suddenly, out of sheer survival instinct, you find yourself looking at your opponent, you'll shoot high at best. More likely, you'll have no idea where your gun is in relation to your opponent and you'll miss him altogether.

That's why so many cops fire shots that miss during an armed confrontation. They're looking at an opponent, but they've been trained to look at their sights.

There's an old saying in the army: "Train the way you fight." For the most part, the army ignores it. But in Delta, the only unit in the entire army on continual war footing, we didn't have the luxury of wasted training time. When the bell rang, we had to come out of the corner not just swinging, but landing killing blows. We had to look at our enemy and hit him—right where we wanted to hit him. Kill him and take him out of the fight before he could cause any harm. In a deadly fight in a room or the cabin of an airplane, we couldn't afford to do anything else.

Initially we fired one round at a time. When we could consistently hit the spot we were looking at (told to look at, told to hit), we increased the distance. When we had that distance down, we moved close to the target again and practiced slapping double taps—two very fast shots—in the same spot. The intention for the double tap is to create a terrible wound that's sure to be fatal.

We did it over and over and over. Soon the fun went out of it, and it became work. And about that time it became painful. The .45 is a powerful pistol with sharp recoil, and the tight grip we used meant we absorbed the full force of the recoil in our hands and arms.

Soon, like everyone else, I had a large painful blister in the web of my thumb from the pounding of the gun in my hand. It would heal just enough at night to really hurt the next day. After a while, the blister turned into a big callus that stayed on my hand for the next eight years. The surest way to identify a Delta Force assault team member is by that telltale callus on his firing hand. They all have one.

Shoot we did. Eight hours a day, thousands of rounds downrange. We shot till our targets were destroyed, and then we put up new ones. When we had the technique down standing in one position, the instructors taught us left and right turning movements. When we had mastered that, we learned to turn our backs to the targets, face about, and shoot on command.

Then we learned to walk and shoot. At first we walked directly toward the target and then parallel to it. Then away from it, spinning and firing on command. We worked in four-man groups, each led by one of the four instructors— Bill, Mike, Bob, or Allen. We changed instructors every day. Our skills increased along with our confidence in one another, and we stood closer and closer to the other members of our team while firing.

Soon we were shooting multiple targets, first in twos and threes, then in larger groups. Next we added "good guy" targets mixed in with the "bad guys." The targets got closer together, and the bad guys were sometimes partially covered by the good guys.

Then we mastered shooting on the run, always closing with the targets, always being aggressive. We would transition from the submachine gun to the pistol, or from the pistol to the submachine gun. Our instructor would load a pistol for us and intentionally induce a malfunction or load only a partial magazine so that we would have to execute a transition to another weapon, a reload drill, or clear a malfunction. Our response to the unexpected had to be routine.

Then we did these things in teams of twos, and then

threes, and then fours. We would engage a group of targets as a team, closing with them and distributing fire while remaining acutely aware of the men adjacent to us, often shooting near them and them near us. The point was to calculate the angle of fire on the move, hitting the bad guys without the rounds going through them and hitting a good guy.

To hit a good guy meant an immediate "Chinese self-criticism drill." Everything stopped and we had to explain to the instructor and our teammates why we had shot a good guy. It wasn't taken lightly and it wasn't funny. Short of shooting a comrade, it was about the worst mistake we could make.

We were training to rescue hostages, and if we couldn't keep from hitting them in a fight, we weren't doing our job. If we were no better than that, then a squad of infantry could do the job. They could just go in and kill everybody.

We worked at this for more than a month. One solid month on the range. At the end of the day, we would put our weapons and equipment on the truck, change into running clothes, and run back to the compound a little more than five miles away. It was a good way to sweat off the intensity of the day. When we got in, we would clean weapons, talk about the day, clean ourselves, go home, and come back to do it again the next day.

Everyone sees rapid improvement in his shooting ability at first. Then he reaches a sort of plateau where improvement seems slow and incremental. After that, every gain is made by working on the finer points of technique. By this time, we were splitting hairs with our shooting.

And then we were introduced to the shooting house, where we'd spend eight hours a day for the next month.

* * *

The shooting house was at the compound. In fact, it was just out the back door from our OTC bay. I had helped build it, putting up drywall just before we started OTC, and the guys ahead of us in the unit were already shooting there several hours a day.

That original shooting house was a simple affair with four rooms, two on each side, and a central corridor down the middle. Each room's lighting could be controlled from the hallway and raised or lowered as needed. Three of the rooms could be set up to resemble almost any type of dwelling, office, or warehouse space. The fourth room was the aircraft room—a section of aircraft fuselage complete with airplane doors, passenger seats, and overhead luggage bins.

The place was ruggedly constructed to withstand the impact of all the bullets and explosives used inside. The door frames in each room were made of heavy timbers and slightly recessed so that we could breach them with explosives and then put up new doors.

There was a central ventilation system to pull out the smoke, but unfortunately, it pulled air in at the bottom of the walls and exhausted through the ceilings, so a lot of lead dust and vapors went right up our noses. We changed the ventilation when we realized the problem, but within a year, several guys had dangerously high concentrations of lead in their systems from the spent bullets and had to limit their time in the shooting house.

The shooting house could be a very eerie place. The day our instructors took us in for an introduction was a real eye-opener. Each room was furnished differently: one like an office, one like a living room, one like an industrial setting—an office or a warehouse—and, of course, one like an aircraft. They looked so real it was weird. The furniture was new, the carpets were clean, and the place was peopled with manikins in natural poses and dress. Some were terrorists, and others were hostages. There were even children. If I hadn't realized before how serious this business was, I sure knew it now.

This was where all of our range work came together. In the shooting house, we added tactics to shooting. The formula became infinitely more complicated and hazardous. Our instructors demonstrated. With live fire.

Our OTC class, all twenty-three of us, was taken into the big room of the shooting house. Some of us were seated on the sofa, some around a card table; more were scattered around the corners, and the rest stood in the center of the room.

Intermingled among us were bad guys—FBI silhouette targets in the shape of a man holding a pistol. Bill, our chief shooting instructor, placed a handheld radio on the table in the center of the room and told us to listen carefully when the radio came on. Then he stepped outside and closed the door.

Seconds later the radio crackled to life with these words: "I have control—Stand by. Five . . . Four . . . Three . . . Two . . . One . . . *Execute! Execute! Execute!*"

What happened next was so fast it was impossible to follow. The room erupted in noise and violent action.

On that first *"Execute!"*, the door to the room blasted open and I could see Allen coming through at a run. At the very instant he came in, something flew from his hand toward the ceiling at the center of the room and exploded. I tried to watch the team as they came in, but my eye—and everyone else's—had been irresistibly drawn to that flying flash-bang.[1] When it exploded above our heads, I hardly heard the pistols and submachine gun going off all around us. I was stunned motionless.

It was over in less than three seconds. Our instructors were posted all about the room. Allen was in one corner and Mike was in the corner diagonally opposite. Bob was just to the left of the door and Bill was just to the right. Smoke hung in the air and I could taste the acrid fumes of the flash-bang in the back of my throat.

Bill looked at Allen and said, "Search."

Weapon at the ready, Allen moved over the sector of the room he had assaulted, checking the "terrorists" for signs of life. Bill covered while Allen checked each target and returned to his position in the corner.

When Allen was back in position, he gave Bill a nod, and Bill shifted his attention to Mike, giving him the same command. Bob covered Mike as Mike checked the "dead," and twice Bob moved a step forward or to the side so that he could easily cover a target while Mike checked it. Mike never stepped in front of an unchecked target in a way that would have prevented Bob from shooting if he had to.

I looked around the room and saw that each "terrorist" had two bullet holes in a vital spot, either the head, the center of the chest, or the throat. *How did they do that with us all around the room and intermingled with the targets?* I thought. It seemed impossible that all those bullets had missed us.

---

[1] A flash-bang is a small explosive grenade that makes a loud noise and a flash of bright light but produces no shrapnel. It's frightening and distracting, but not deadly.

Someone should have been hit. But we were all whole and unperforated. It was unreal.

Bill asked, "Did everybody see what happened during the assault?"

"Heck no, Bill," somebody croaked. "All we saw was that flash-bang and then you guys were in here."

"That's the way it's supposed to work," replied Bill. "Now we'll do it again at a walking pace and I'll explain it as we go along.

"Under normal conditions, we would've blown the door with explosives, but in this case, it would've been too much of a distraction."

As Bill spoke, Allen walked through the room in demonstration.

"The first man in the room, the number-one man, threw the flash-bang," said Bill, "and made an instant decision to turn left. He did that because the left side was the 'heavy side' of the room, meaning there were more people on that side than on the other. It could also mean that it was a longer side of the room—you'll learn more about that later. The number-one man always goes to the heavy side, which usually means the more dangerous side."

Allen was walking the left side of the room, simulating shooting the targets he had engaged on the live-fire run-through.

"Staying close to the wall, he goes down that side of the room, engaging any targets in that area. He turns at the corner and goes down that wall, still engaging targets. He halts at the far corner and faces back into the room."

We all looked at Allen.

"On the first time through, did anyone follow Allen until he stopped in his corner?" Bill asked innocently, though he obviously knew the answer.

We all shook our heads.

"Why not?" he asked.

Several people said they'd been distracted by the flashbang. Guy Harmon gave another reason. "I tried to watch him," he said, "but instead I noticed Mike, coming in right on top of Allen, but Mike turned right and that drew my attention away."

"Did you see him shoot?" Bill asked.

"No, I didn't," said Guy. "I knew he was shooting, but I was making myself small and covering up. My mind was on surviving."

Bill nodded. "OK," he said, and then he continued. "Mike came in right on top of Allen, but he turned right when Allen went left. Mike immediately engaged the targets on the far wall opposite the door, then went down the wall to the first corner, turned, and came to a halt, watching into the corner further down the wall, and out into the center of the room."

Mike walked through each step as Bill narrated.

"Do you see what happened here? It's impossible to keep an eye on movement in opposite directions. If you're the terrorist, you can't keep up with what's going on because your attention is divided—and fatally so. But the assaulter is only concerned with what's in front of him in his sector of the room.

"Who saw me and Bob as we entered the room?" he asked.

No one had. When the shooting had stopped, I'd noticed

that they were in the room on each side of the doorway. I had felt their presence, but hadn't seen them until the action had stopped.

Bill went on with his explanation. "Rather than pile in right on top of the first two men, we hesitated a split second before entering the room. That way, the attention of the terrorists was no longer on the door but on the two men in the room, who were still on the move. With attention drawn away from the door—numbers one and two men kept moving—we came in unnoticed.

"I went to the heavy side and started engaging targets in that area to assist the number-one man. I worked from the center of the room to the left. Bob stepped to the other side and worked from the center to the right." As he said this, they positioned themselves as described. It was perfect.

"Look at us now. Look at our positions and the areas we're covering. There's not a square inch of this room that's not covered by fire and observation. If a piece of furniture presents an obstacle to one man, at least two others can see—and shoot—around it. We have completely dominated the room. We own it and everyone in it.

"Had you men actually been hostages," Bill went on, "as team leader, I would've started talking to you as soon as the shooting stopped. We want the hostages to stay calm and comply with our commands. We'll ask if they know of anyone or anything else in the room that is still a threat to their safety. We want to know if any terrorists are hiding in the room or among the hostages, and whether or not there are any explosives. But the last thing you ask is, 'Are there any bombs in the place?' We don't want to start a stampede."

As if the flash-bangs and submachine guns weren't enough.

"When we've determined everything is under control in here, I'll render a situation report to the troop commander. I'll tell him the room is clear, ask for medical assistance if we need it, and tell him we're prepared to evacuate the hostages. We'll continue to talk to and engage the attention of the hostages until they are moved out to the hostage holding area, where they will be initially questioned and identified.

"When the hostages are out, we brief ourselves on what happened in the room. In turn, each team member demonstrates and explains his actions in the room. He'll recount where he went, who he shot, how many rounds he fired and where, and he'll account for each shot fired. Not until we all know exactly what the team did inside the room will I report to the troop commander that I'm ready to turn the room over to troop control. The only exception to this would be an emergency evacuation, caused by, say, an uncontrolled fire or the discovery of explosives."

Jimmy Masters raised his hand to ask a question. Jimmy, a Creek Indian from Oklahoma, was one of the sharpest men in the class. When he had a question or a comment, it was always valuable.

Bill acknowledged him with a nod and said, "Jim, I'm going to ask you, and everyone else, to hold the questions for now. We're going to take a break and reconvene back in the classroom. Colonel Beckwith wants to speak to you. Then we'll answer all your questions and take it from there. The shooting house is going to be your full-time home for the next month or so. OK, that's it. Classroom in fifteen minutes."

And we were dismissed.

Even though I had seen it up close, the room assault was hard to believe. The suddenness of it was astounding. One moment all was calm, then hell erupted, and just as suddenly, calm returned. There was a mental factor at work here that intrigued me.

The assault team had exploded into action when they had assaulted the room, but when it had concluded, they had immediately gone back to a calm, controlled mental state. It appeared seamless. They didn't have to stop after their explosion of intensity to regain their composure; they went smoothly from one mode to the other. They knew when to rush, and when to go slow, but their self-control never deserted them. They never became overly or visibly excited, as most men would have.

I could now see where all those shooting drills were leading us. If we stopped right now, we would be amazing combat shooters—infinitely better than any other military unit I knew of. But the next phase of training would take us to an altogether different level.

And deep in the core of my being was a kernel of dread: *Would I be able to do that? Would I be able to shoot that close to another person and run the risk of killing an innocent hostage or one of my mates?*

The honest answer was—not yet. My skills were close, but my confidence wasn't.

CHAPTER**EIGHT**

"Gentlemen, the unit commander."

We jumped to our feet and the position of attention as Colonel Beckwith swept down the center aisle of the classroom like a hungry bear headed for a bee tree. This was the first time Beckwith had addressed us as a class.

"Sit down, men, sit down," he growled, and waved us back into our seats. He stood at the front of the classroom with his fists in his hip pockets, and for a full minute, he looked us over with a penetrating glare.

He looked and sounded a lot like the old cowboy actor Chill Wills—but in a malevolent way. His gravelly voice rumbled from deep within his chest. Like the rest of us, he wasn't in uniform. He had on dirty suede desert boots and wore his khaki trousers slung low under his belly. Up top he wore an open-necked blue oxford shirt underneath a navy blazer. He looked as if the clothes had been thrown at him and more or less landed in the right places. He also looked as if he could not have cared less. And this from a man who later hired a fashion consultant to teach us how to dress. Finally he spoke again.

"Well," he drawled. "You boys just got a little taste of what we're all about, eh? We ain't sellin' shoes or makin' cornflakes 'round here. It's serious bidness we talkin' about. You got ta kill and ya got to be dang good at it . . . 'cause we ain't takin' no prisoners. We ain't sendin' no terrorists to prison just so they buddies kin take more hostages to git 'em loose. No sir, we gonna drop 'em dead on the ground and make martyrs out of 'em. That's the best way to go about it.

"And you cain't be shootin' no hostages while ye doin' it!" he thundered. "I ain't gonna be 'splainin' to the president why we went in and shot up a bunch of innocent folks we was 'sposed to be rescuin'."

Beckwith had slipped into the Georgia Cracker dialect he favored when speaking to us on serious matters—or when he was angry. As I came to know him, I realized it was an affectation he used for dramatic effect. Beckwith was in deadly earnest about the subject of terrorism, but he was always a showman.

"So ye got to be good and ye got to be smart," he continued as he paced back and forth across the front of the room. "I'll take care of the luck."

He stopped dead center and leaned toward us, a wild smile creeping across his face.

"And I'll tell ye what you're working towards," he went on. "Soon's you boys finish OTC we'll have enough bodies here to officially form this unit. Then we gonna take about six months to do our unit training and after that I'm gonna tell the president we ready to go. And then you better grab yer tails 'cause I'm gonna keep ye busy. I tell ye, things gonna be so good—we gonna do such great things, it'll be like pickin' up diamonds from right off the ground. Yes sirree, diamonds big as mule turds.

144

"So y'all pay attention to what Bill and his team are teachin' ye. This phase of training is about to git dangerous and I cain't afford to lose none of ye yet. Awright, Bill, they yerz. Carry on."

And with that he launched himself down the aisle and out the door so fast we barely made it to our feet before he was gone.

Well, that was entertaining. Diamonds big as mule turds, eh? We'll have to see about that. One man's diamond is another man's turd. And he can't afford to lose any of us yet? Hmmm. I wonder when he can afford to lose some of us.

But he was certainly right about one thing: the next phase of training had the potential to be very, very dangerous. However, I had every confidence in our crew of instructors. They had gotten us to this point in a masterful fashion, and I was certain they would bring us through the next hurdles.

We spent the rest of the morning in the classroom while Allen diagrammed the steps of room combat on the blackboard. He drew the sequence of each team member's movements and actions just the way Bill had outlined it when talking through their steps for us in the shooting house.

On the board, it was easy to see how the room was divided into overlapping sectors of coverage. In the room, it hadn't been so readily visible.

Speed, surprise, and violence of action. Those were the keys to success and survival—those and the ability to shoot what we intended to shoot and nothing else. We were not just going to go into harm's way. We were going to charge down harm's throat, grab a handful of his guts, and turn him inside out.

The individual attributes of an aggressive and adventurous spirit were such fundamental requirements for this work that it was taken for granted that each man had what was necessary. Selection had seen to that. Now we were just adding the skills.

We started in the shooting house as we had on the range: first walking through without weapons, then with weapons but dry-firing. Next walking through while live-firing with one target, then with added targets. We increased our speed until we could move at a full run.

It was exciting. Standing outside the door to a room in the ready position, muscles tensing, wound up like a coiled spring, guns going off in the other rooms. Bill, Mike, Allen, or Bob holding the handle to the door, counting down with voice and fingers: *"Three . . . Two . . . One . . . EXECUTE, EXECUTE, EXECUTE!"*

You blast inside and immediately make a turn left or right. Sometimes a target is right in your face—right inside the doorway. You have to shoot on the move, shoot and keep moving at full speed, and keep shooting until all targets are taken out. Then you assess the room for other dangers, other threats. Your heart is still pounding from that burst of speed and energy, but your mind has to remain calm and detached. It's as if you have to observe yourself and the scene from outside your body—from a spot on the ceiling where you can take it all in with a fish-eye lens.

Soon it feels good; it feels fluid. You start to clear the room with a style that feels automatic. If a target is in your sector, you shoot it without even looking to see the hits—because you knew where the shots went before they were fired. Your pistol or submachine gun follows your eyes while your mind ranges ahead. You can feel the gun moving in your hands, sense and count the shots as they're fired, but you never really hear the sounds of the shots going off.

Next we added hostage targets to the equation. Then our instructors switched to cartoon targets that sometimes held weapons and sometimes didn't. That caused a little hesitation and embarrassment at first, but soon it made no difference at all. We shot either because the targets held weapons or because the targets were identified as "bad" (whether they had weapons or not) just as the instructor flung open the door and we hurled ourselves inside to do battle.

Then we started working in pairs, two men in at a time, the first man taking the heavy side, the second man going to the other side of the room. That added a whole new dimension and feel to the exercise: hearing and feeling the fire from a partner, knowing that the angles of fire were shifting and changing and that a "friendly"—one of us—was in the room. The angles and elevations of our shots took on added importance. We didn't want to hit a mate, but sometimes we would miss each other by inches with the rounds we fired.

Next we added "teammate down" drills, learning how to pick up a partner's side of the room if he was shot and incapacitated or if his weapons malfunctioned. We shifted from room to room and partner to partner, and each scenario was different from the one before. When we were fluent in clearing a room as a two-man team, we started rotating through the aircraft room.

To clear a section of an aircraft cabin, two men would

rush down the aisle, looking for all the world like a set of deadly Siamese twins, the lead man low and his partner right over his shoulder, one clearing left and the other right. Head shots were the norm because that was all that could usually be seen of a target over the tops of the seats and the heads of the "passengers." To make those shots while running at full speed—without touching a hostage—was the most difficult task imaginable. All our shots passed within a hair's distance of a friendly, but there was no excuse for so much as grazing a hostage. To do so meant the dreaded public self-criticism drill.

When we could function well as two-man teams, we formed four-man teams. We shifted around the shooting house between rooms and team members. An instructor was in charge of each room and we rotated from station to station. Every room presented a different situation and a new problem to overcome.

When clearing the aircraft room as a four-man team, we would enter the cabin by the over-wing emergency exit and immediately break into a pair of two-man teams—one team clearing forward and the other team behind. We worked on emergency evacuations and moving stunned and frightened passengers with a minimum of effort and fuss.

I felt confident—not only in my own abilities, but also in the abilities of all my comrades. There wasn't a single man in the group I had the slightest hesitation about going into a room and letting loose a storm of gunfire with.

About that time, Bill made an announcement.

"You've all done well, guys, and you've come a long way in a very short time. You're actually much farther along than we were in the same period of training."

It was hard to imagine those four men ever being novices at close-quarter battle.

"But now we're going to take a break from the shooting house. I'm going to turn you over to Dave Donaldson. He and his crew will be in charge of your breaching training. Some of it is mechanical, but most of it is concerned with explosives. You'll be working with Dave for a couple of weeks, and then you'll come back to the shooting house to apply what you've learned. Give Dave and his team the attention you've given us, and we'll see you again later. . . ." He paused.

"Just make sure you come back with all your fingers."

And with those words, Bill smiled for the first time.

Mentally and physically, Dave Donaldson was as perfectly proportioned a human being as I had ever known. He wasn't quite average height, maybe five foot seven, but he had the presence of a large man. He was an old Special Forces engineer, a demolitions specialist, and he knew more about the practical use of explosives than any man alive.

That didn't come across because he talked about what he knew, but because he could show someone what to do and how to do it. With all ten fingers.

Just as there are no old bold pilots, there are no old fearless demo men. You have to handle explosives the way you would handle a large bad-tempered rattlesnake. You never take the snake for granted, and you never, ever let your attention wander.

With demolitions, you check everything over not just once, but three times. And you never take shortcuts. If you do, you may become atomized pink goo on the nearest unde-molished hard surface.

We were already experienced in the use of standard military explosives. For the combat infantryman, the Ranger, and the Special Forces soldier, explosives are just another tool for making a hole in something or knocking it over efficiently. And if we can harm the enemy in the process, so much the better. But Dave was going to teach us breaching—getting into a place while causing the least damage and using the least material.

Dave and his crew were already pretty knowledgeable about the mechanical end of the spectrum, but to prepare for the course, they talked to the real experts: convicted cat burglars and escape artists serving long-term sentences in maximum-security prisons.

The prisoners really warmed up once they understood that they were helping a secret military organization by divulging their techniques and unique abilities. As a result we all came away impressed and better informed. It was sort of funny: Those guys plied their skills, and the government sent them to prison. We plied the same skills on behalf of that very same government and got paid to do it.

We started by learning to quietly break into buildings. We learned to scale the outsides of buildings to get to upper floors, descend to lower ones, or drop unharmed from roofs. Using a push drill[1] and a straightened coat hanger, we opened window latches from the outside. Then we went to work on door locks. We learned about the various styles

[1] Push drill: a small handheld drill that works automatically when pushed.

of locks and their internal workings. We jimmied locks, picked locks, and made duplicate keys. Once we got through the locks, we defeated inside security chains with a rubber band, a paper clip, and a thumbtack. For sliding bolts, we went back to the drill and coat hanger.

We opened padlocks with fingernail-shaped pieces of metal cut from a beer can. (You may have noticed that I'm not explaining how to do all this. You'll have to learn that somewhere else.) We finished every day with a practical exam: an array of different locks to defeat within a set time period. This included escaping from handcuffs.

We used any tool that could help us break in to any place.

We became proficient with cutting torches, metal-cutting saws, jacks, cranes, hoists, and the famous Jaws of Life.

Next came vehicles. We opened locked doors and defeated locked steering columns. We started vehicles with hot-wire kits made under Dave's expert tutelage. These became part of the car-theft equipment we kept with us ever after. It's probably not much of a surprise these days, but a decent car thief with a three-tool theft kit can get into and start your car about as fast as you can with your keys. So can a Delta operator.

We spent days on the demolition range reviewing the basics and doing simple work with standard explosives. We made craters with dynamite and cut trees with TNT to form obstacles. We built and detonated things such as earmuff charges[2] to destroy bridge supports, and we fashioned C-4[3]

[2] Earmuff charges: small explosive charges placed on opposite sides of a concrete structure and detonated simultaneously.
[3] C-4 is the military standard plastic explosive.

into special shapes to cut railroad rails, I beams, and thick steel rods. Using specialized shaped charges made from wine bottles and C-4, we cut into safes. We blew up first a large delivery van and then a house, using a bag of flour, a pad of steel wool, and four ounces of TNT.

We made easy-to-use, safe-to-handle explosives after a trip to the local hardware store. An ammonium nitrate charge, for example, came from two hundred pounds of fertilizer, ten quarts of motor oil, and five pounds of dynamite. Bury a charge like that in the ground and you can make a crater thirty feet wide and fifteen feet deep.

Then we worked with specialized breaching charges. Those were explosive materials that allowed us to make precise surgical cuts into the doors and walls of any building or other man-made structure. Using those charges, we could slash our way to the inside of any target in a manner that was safe not only to us but to the hostages inside.

Now we were in business. No barrier could keep us out. After our training period with Dave, we headed back to the shooting house to put our newly acquired skills to practical application. With all the fingers we started with.

For the next three days, Bill and his team put us through a series of tactical situations in the shooting house. Each drill required us to explosively penetrate the door of the room we were assaulting—and to do it safely. At least, safely for us.

When we hit three rooms simultaneously, it made some kind of a blast. One charge going off in the confines of the shooting house hallway was really something, but three going off at the same time was like a rocket at liftoff. The noise, shock wave, and fireballs from three charges detonating together were horrendous. And we were standing right in the middle of it all. The lead man of each team was only inches from the door charge when it exploded, and the only protective gear we wore in those early days were foam earplugs. Only later did we get protective eyewear, and later still we added protective vests. Live and learn. Thankfully, we lived while we learned.

On day three of that week, we got a real treat: we went out to the range for some joint demolition/shooting work with the unit snipers.

The facade of a two-story building had been built downrange to allow the snipers to shoot targets that rapidly appeared and disappeared in the windows and doorways. For this training session, the long gunners guided our movements to the moving crisis point by radio, telling us when it was clear to move, and halting us when the target was present. On our final approach to the target, and as we placed our charges on the doors, they covered our every movement by fire.

Together we worked on coordinated assaults. That was when the assault teams had approached the target undetected, had placed charges on the breach points, and were in position for the assault. When all teams signaled ready, the commander took over and set the assault in motion with the radio command:

"I have control—Stand by. Five . . . Four . . . Three . . . Two . . . One . . . Execute! Execute! Execute!"

On the count of two, the snipers fired on any exposed terrorists, right over the heads of the assaulters crouched under the windows. On the count of one, the charges were blown. At "Execute," the assaulters launched themselves into the room and unleashed hell.

Then we worked on an important variation of the coordinated assault. We made our approach as before and put everything in place; then all teams would signal ready. Then . . . nothing.

The commander would hold us in position. Or start and stop the countdown. Or call us completely off the target and back to the assault position. It was an exercise to teach us that we were a disciplined force; once we were *switched on*, we could also be *switched off*. But it's difficult to back off a target once you're ready to go—even in training. It's like a dog being called away from a cat he's just cornered; he might do it, but he ain't got to like it.

We did each of these assaults again after dark, using the night as our principal ally. It made everything easier for us. Wearing night-vision goggles, we could see in the dark and shoot just as accurately as in the daylight. And a benefit of the instinctive shooting technique was that even without goggles, we shot as well in the dark as in the light.

We finished late that night and were back at the Ranch—the unit compound—cleaning weapons when Bill made an announcement.

"Guys, you all did well. The snipers told me before we left how much they enjoyed working with you today, and you can bet that Colonel Beckwith will know about it by tomorrow.

"We have just one main shooting house training objective left to accomplish during this phase, and it happens tomorrow and the next day. Remember how you were introduced to the shooting house that first day? Well, now it's your turn."

The room went silent.

"Each of you will take turns playing the hostage and sitting in the hot seat while your mates conduct a live-fire assault. You will be a hostage four times. You will also rotate through every position on the assault team. Each assault will initiate with an explosive breach. Meet in the classroom for the mission briefing at ten hundred hours. Get a good night's sleep. See you in the morning."

And with a nonchalant wave of his hand, he dismissed us.

This is going to be some final exam, I thought as I finished cleaning my pistol. *Pass, and it's just another training day. Screw up, shoot and kill a friend, and you fail. That's a high penalty for flunking a test.*

I looked around the arms room at my friends and comrades. *Do I trust my ability and skills enough to hurl deadly missiles within millimeters of their heads? One misstep, one flinch, and it could be catastrophic. My little girl plays with the children of the guys in this room. Yeah, Bill. Get a good night's sleep. That's a good one. I'll never close my eyes tonight,* I thought as I put my gear away and walked to the parking lot.

Now it was my turn. I was sitting in a leather armchair in one of the rooms of the shooting house. The place was furnished like a living room with sofas and chairs, coffee and end tables, mirrors, pictures, and bookcases. There were even books on the shelves.

The lighting was dim. Manikins and paper targets were

155

positioned about the room. Some held guns and some were empty-handed. They were the terrorists and I was their hostage. There was an armed manikin crouched behind me, positioned with one hand on my neck and the other on my shoulder, pointing a pistol at the door. Another terrorist stood on my other side, pointing a submachine gun at my head.

Within the next ten minutes, the door would be blown in and four of my classmates would assault the room using the close-quarter battle techniques we had learned. Within three seconds of the explosion, they would have to kill the terrorists, gain positive control of the room, and rescue me. Bullets would rain throughout the room, and someone would be firing live rounds within inches of my head. If they missed a single terrorist or hit me by mistake, the team would fail this phase of training.

I sincerely wanted them to pass the exam.

My team and I had successfully passed the first test that morning. Marty Johnson had been the hostage, and he had only blinked when a pair of double taps from my .45-caliber pistol knocked the heads off the terrorist manikins close beside him. Then we changed positions within the team and made three more assaults in different rooms with other comrades occupying the hot seat.

Now that I was here, I realized it was harder to be the shooter than the hostage. To be in the assault team required great confidence in your abilities. To be the hostage required faith in your comrades. It was easier to think of being shot than of shooting a mate.

As the minutes ticked by slowly, I thought about the long, hard path we'd taken to this point. We had spent untold hours on the range and in the shooting house and had fired hundreds of thousands of rounds to get here, to this room, to this chair.

I heard an explosion down the hall, then the immediate stutter of pistols and submachine guns in another room. The firing was over in just a few seconds.

I hope that went well. I glanced down at my watch. *The assault should be any time now. I sure hope these guys pass their test; I most sincerely do.* The door exploded with a flash and a clap, and a shock wave hit me like a punch in the face.

I saw the team hurling themselves into the room, saw the splashes of fire from the muzzles of their guns, and felt the slap of air as bullets flew by my face. But I can't honestly say that I heard any one distinct sound or that my brain registered any one distinct image. It happened so fast, so suddenly, that even though I was expecting it, it was so completely over-powering that my system was unable to respond until it was all over. The ferocity of the attack stunned me. It was like a strike of lightning—a pure and elemental force.

J.T. was the team leader. As he gave commands to his team to conduct the search, I unfroze enough to turn in my chair and check the terrorist over my shoulder. The manikin's head was lying on the floor a few feet away, with one hole just under his right cheek and another slightly in front of his ear.

The terrorist on my other side had a pair of holes at the base of his throat. The rest of the manikins and cartoon targets around the room had at least two hits in the kill zone; some had four where the three and four men had added their shots to an already hit target.

When the team finished their room search, J.T. gave me a toothy grin from under his lush mustache. "You OK, Bubba?" he asked as he looked me over from head to toe.

Allen had just stepped into the room and he looked me over along with the targets.

"Yeah, J.T., I'm fine," I replied.

Allen finished his scrutiny of the room. "All right, boys, that's a go. Now do it three more times and you're shooting house graduates. But don't let that pressure you or anything." He smiled as he marked his clipboard. "Paste up the targets, put a new head on that dummy, and get ready for the next run-through. J.T., have a seat and make yourself comfortable. It's your turn in the barrel."

"Give me your equipment, J.T.," I said, cheerful again as I got up from the chair. "I'll put it down by the reload table in the hallway. And don't worry about a thing, old buddy. We'll be gentle—I know it's your first time."

"Yeah, thanks" was all he said as we cleared out of the room. He was uncharacteristically quiet while we hung a new door on the hinges and locked it into place.

It all came off without a hitch. Everyone had multiple turns as a hostage and as an assaulter with a live hostage in the room. Nobody was hurt and no targets were missed. And the confidence that that life-or-death final examination gave us—in ourselves as much as in our mates—stuck with us for life. I trusted myself and I trusted my comrades in a way that was unshakable. From that point on, no matter the situation, no matter how dangerous, we would prevail.

I believed that to the core of my being. I still do.

* * *

"We do more observing and reporting than we do shooting, so perhaps we would be better called observer-reporters than snipers," explained the long gun chief, Larry Freedman.

"In fact," he went on, "when dealing with outsiders, we use the term 'sniper/observer' and not 'sniper' because so much of what we do is scene observation and collection of immediate intelligence. And that's what you guys are going to get a taste of this week."

Master Sergeant Larry Freedman loved life like few other human beings I'd met. He was intensely interested in people and always amused with life's surprises. Years later, after retiring from the army and while working for the CIA, he would become the first American killed during America's intervention in Somalia.

"Some of you will be selected for assignment to a sniper troop when you've finished OTC," said Freedman. "But all of you have to understand how we do our business. At one time or another on a site, every one of you will pull duty in the TOC—Tactical Operations Center—so it's vitally important you learn our reporting methods and procedures. Also, as you saw on the range last week, snipers will often overwatch your movement and guide assault teams to the target. Or an assault will be sniper initiated.

"But more than any of that jazz," he said, jabbing his finger at us, "we don't want you getting in our way and screwing up a shot—and you sure don't want us shooting you." By this time, he was wearing a huge grin that threw deep wrinkles across his face.

Larry Freedman had a head full of wiry, prematurely gray

hair that he was inordinately proud of and a great thick mustache. Permanent laugh lines radiated from the corners of his eyes. He would often laugh so hard at some antic he had witnessed or a joke he was telling that tears would run dripping down his cheeks.

Larry worked hard to maintain the chiseled Mr. America body that had helped earn him his code name, Superman, but he was also a super man in many other ways. He looked after his snipers as if they were his own flesh and blood, and whenever anybody in the unit needed a helping hand or some wise counsel, it was usually Larry who knew what to do or say.

He was also known for the battles he had with Colonel Beckwith whenever Charlie tried to interfere with what Larry thought was best and right for his snipers. The yelling matches they had were legend in the unit. Years later, while he and I were huddled together in some godforsaken spot on the globe, Larry told me that Beckwith had fired him on six separate occasions.

"But I'm still here," he crowed, "three commanders later." The fights they had were merely lovers' spats; Beckwith thought the world of Larry, and Larry thought the same of our commander.

That day was our introduction to the world Larry loved so much, the world of the sniper.

"First we'll spend a couple of days getting down the basics of reporting," he said, "and then we'll go out to the range and run some practical exercises. You guys are going to enjoy this, I guarantee. Now let me introduce your instructor, Branislav Urbanski. He'll be your guide the rest of the week."

Branislav Urbanski was an extraordinary character, and he, too, became one of my best friends. Branislav had escaped from Poland in the late 1960s and made his way to America when he was just a teenager. Once here, he discovered that the fastest way to an American citizenship was via the military, so he joined up. His use of the English language and view of American culture had been learned in the U.S. Army, specifically in the old separate Ranger companies, and because of that, both were a little off-center of the prevailing societal norms.

Branislav was one of our premier snipers, and now he took us under his wing of knowledge and ability and explained things we would have to know, starting with how to look at a building and report what we saw.

On the face of it, that sounds like a pretty simple procedure. But with sniper teams posted all around a crisis point, it takes some hard-and-fast reference points to keep the situation from turning into pure chaos. Branislav taught us how to impose order on reporting. The idea is simplicity itself.

Buildings are given a color code to designate specific sides. The front is designated white. The back of the target, black. The target's left is red and its right is green.

Floors or levels are given phonetic alphabet designations, in ascending order. Thus the first floor is labeled Alpha, the second Bravo, the third Charlie, and so on. (Yes, some buildings have more floors than the alphabet has letters, and we had a means of handling that.) All openings in the building, whether doorways or windows, were numbered on their respective floors from left to right.

For example, if I was observing the front of the building

and saw something happen in the sixth window on the seventh floor, I would record and report the location as follows:

"White, Golf, Six."

Back at the sniper TOC, the information would be logged and plotted on a map of the target called the target schematic. All other sniper teams would immediately know what happened and where, and as soon as I said, 'white,' the teams on the other sides of the building would know that it was something outside their own zones of observation.

We used the same means of identification on planes, trains, buses, and boats. In fact, it was adapted from the method of marking the sides of ships and planes with navigation lights: red for the left, or port, side and green for the right, or starboard, side of the vessel.

Brani pointed out that by patient, careful observation and reporting, the snipers could build up an extremely valuable body of information on a terrorist crisis scene. Details such as which areas were used and, just as important, which areas were not. The location of hostages. The actions the terrorists would take during periods of heightened tension. Their leadership, rest schedule, and a million other things that helped build accurate profiles of them as individuals.

Delta Force snipers are chosen only after extensive additional psychological testing and evaluation. There are a number of attributes we look for in a sniper, and there are two of paramount importance to avoid.

The first characteristic to look out for is what we called the Texas Tower Syndrome, referencing Charles Whitman's massacre of fourteen people from the bell tower of the University of Texas in 1966. That characteristic manifests itself when a sniper starts shooting and can't stop. It just feels so good—such an overwhelming sense of power—that he can't turn it off when there are no more legitimate targets left. And he'll continue to shoot anyone in sight. It is a very real compulsion and I've heard its siren call in my own ear.

The second characteristic takes a much different, more understandable form. This one we termed the Munich Massacre Syndrome.

Think of it like this. A sniper spends most of his time watching. Observing. Getting to know his targets. Through his high-power spotting scope, a sniper can see the features on the faces of the terrorists as clearly as if he were in the room with them. He sees them when they smile, and sneeze, and eat a sandwich, and get drowsy, and as they manifest all the other little things that identify each of us as uniquely human.

But they don't know he can see them. They have no idea where he is. They don't even know he exists. The terrorists represent no personal threat to the sniper whatsoever. They are far away. They can't harm him. They can't kill him. And as the sniper spends hour after hour observing his targets through his spotting scope, he gets to know the people he is watching as human beings and he becomes intimate with them. And then, when the order to shoot is given, he can't do it. He can't kill these people he has come to know, these people who are no threat to his life.

That's what happened at the Munich Olympic Massacre in 1972. When the order was given to shoot the Black September terrorists who had taken eleven Israeli athletes hostage, the German police sharpshooters couldn't pull the trigger. They had observed the hostage-takers for such a long time and developed such a sense of empathy for them that they couldn't bring themselves to kill people they felt they now knew. As a result the terrorists were then able to kill the Israeli Olympic athletes under their control.

The psychological niche in which can be found the man who can shoulder aside these two behavioral opposites is very narrow. The ideal is a man who, from the safety of long range, can kill when it is required, but is immune to the impulse to continue killing when the situation is resolved. A man whose psyche is strong and so fundamentally rooted in a personal philosophy or religion that he doesn't suffer unduly from taking human life under appropriate conditions. The snipers of Delta Force are decent, thoughtful, intelligent, and unshakable men. By their demeanor, they could easily be taken for academics—very fit, powerful, and deadly academics, perhaps, but professorial just the same.

After our talk, the class divided in half and Branislav took my group into the other classroom to begin our practical exercise. On a large table in the middle of the classroom was an eight-story building in miniature, so perfectly detailed it could have been part of a movie set. It had windows and doorways, wide canopied primary entrances, fire escapes, a rooftop garden, and an outdoor restaurant.

Inside the hotel, as we called it, lights could be turned on and off in various rooms. There were even miniature cardboard cutouts of people, some of whom were armed, which could be made to appear and disappear by a series of strings running up through the bottom. Outside there were a few sidewalks and trees, and cars and trucks parked in the adjacent streets.

Branislav gave us the instructions for the training session. Half of us were positioned around the room in observer positions that gave all-around coverage of the building. At each position were a notebook and pen, a pair of binoculars, a camera with a telephoto lens, a compass, and a radio.

Larry Freedman had taken the other half of the class to another room, where they would establish and man a sniper TOC. Some would operate the radios in the TOC, others would transcribe the received data, and still others would plot the reported activity on a sketch of the building drawn from data radioed in by the observers. When film started to come in from the observers, other students would develop it in the sniper "Flyaway" darkroom set up in another room. The photos would be posted along with the building sketches to help construct useful information as the situation developed.

Then each group settled in and set to work. From our observer positions, we had to label the sides of the building and work on individual sketches of the sides we were assigned. We immediately began taking photos of the site, but as Branislav explained, neither sketches nor exposed film would be sent back to the TOC for several hours. Instead, the TOC would have to build its initial picture of the site from our verbal reports over the radio.

Brani came over to my position, and I asked him why we didn't immediately send sketches and exposed film back to the TOC. It seemed to me that it was especially needed just after arrival on the scene. He was ready for me.

Two reasons, he explained. One, because he wanted the guys manning the sniper TOC to produce a picture of the site based upon our radioed reports; it was a good way to get on the same page and to practice radio discipline.

Second, in the first flush of setting up at a site, people were so busy that there usually wasn't a man to spare running back and forth between the various observer positions. And sometimes, depending on the target, we couldn't move between positions without the risk of being spotted. In that case movement took place only after dark. (Remember, all of this took place before digital cameras and computers made instant visual communication possible. Observation techniques have evolved to make the most of technology. And not just today's technology, but tomorrow's.)

We stayed in our positions until six o'clock that evening, when we broke for the day and both groups reunited to compare notes. It was uncanny what the guys in the TOC had accomplished. The first prints from the film we had finally sent back were just coming out of the darkroom, but the target sketch they'd produced—solely from verbal reports—was amazingly accurate.

Larry summed up the day for us: "Guys, the whole point in what takes place, both here in the TOC and out on-site, is to build a body of information you can use to make the best possible decision about when, where, and how to conduct an assault. There is no such thing as a matter too small to be reported and logged. There is no such thing as too much intelligence. We will do everything in our power to make the assaulter's job easier. If we can resolve a situation solely by sniper fire, so much the better. But no matter what, we want to tip the odds in favor of the short gunners when they have to hit the place.

"Since the cat's out of the bag now with our miniature building, we'll go out to the range for the rest of the week and do the same thing we did today using the facade. The group that was in the TOC this afternoon will be on the line, and you other guys will be the TOC bunnies tomorrow. And since there are no questions"—he smiled—"I'll see you all here in the morning."

I thoroughly enjoyed that week with Larry and his crew. I gained a whole new appreciation for what the long gunners did and how they went about it. I realized that shooting *was* only a part of what they did—a vital part, to be sure, but not the only part. And I made some new lifelong friends. Yeah, that was a good week.

More and more I was beginning to feel as if we were part of the unit. We were still some months from being full-fledged operators, but I felt confident we could function well if called upon.

CHAPTER**NINE**

"The toughest thing we're ever going to have to do is recover a terrorist-held airplane,"[1] explained Colonel Beckwith. "We've been working on how to go about it, and so have the British, the Germans, the French, and the Israelis. But so far, nobody has a real good grip on the problem. But it's a problem we've got to solve, and we've got to solve it soon."

Charlie was dressed in a rather presentable fashion that day—and so were the rest of us. We had been told to be in casual dress attire, and we had also been given an order against chewing tobacco in the classroom while this particular visitor was with us. The colonel obviously wanted our guest to form a favorable impression of the unit, and that meant we all had to do our part. We didn't want to come across as a bunch of knuckle-draggers.

"You're going to spend a few days here in the classroom with some visitors and then go down to Atlanta this weekend

---

[1] In the years before September 11, terrorists didn't fly airplanes into buildings. They took airplanes hostage in the air and on the ground and used human beings as a bartering tool for demands.

for a visit the Federal Aviation Administration has helped us arrange with Delta Air Lines. Delta has agreed to let us conduct research and training on planes they have in for scheduled maintenance. This will be our first real chance at working with a civil air carrier, so the whole outfit will be coming down too. We want to make the most of this opportunity.

"I want to remind you again that all of our guests are here under our nonattribution policy. Whatever they share with us is for our use only. We don't divulge their identities, and whatever they say stays right here in the unit. So be smart, pay attention, and give a big hand to our guest, Mr. X of the Federal Aviation Administration."

Beckwith led the applause as our visitor made his way to the front of the classroom. Charlie Beckwith was a master at this sort of thing. He knew that our future depended on the goodwill and help of some of the other government agencies, and he was shrewd enough about human nature to know how to go about gaining that support. He invited people from the highest and most influential levels of government to visit the unit or to be guest speakers.

We took them to the range and the shooting house for live-fire demonstrations—some of them even sat in the hot seat. We let them shoot a few guns and fire off an explosive charge, showed them all sorts of "secret" stuff, and told them they were some of the few outsiders *ever* to see any of this. We'd let them share a meal with the guys in the mess hall, swear them—as new "associate members" of the unit—to undying secrecy, and send them on their happy way home with excited memories of everything they'd seen and done.

Everybody likes to be in on a secret, so by the end of the

visit, we would have a new ally. Then our guest would whisper to a few people about what he had seen and done down with that secret outfit at Fort Bragg, and before long, other people who deemed themselves important would angle for an invitation.

This sort of thing would pay big dividends for the unit in the years to come, and the reality was we always learned something valuable from our guests. Our current visitor was a case in point. He was a very high-ranking official of the FAA, and the information he gave us about aircraft hijacking incidents and the things aircrews were trained to do if hijacked was invaluable.

Coupled with what we learned from the FBI's training academy group the following day, this revealed a very distinct line of demarcation between the authority of the FAA and the authority of the FBI when it came to responsibility for a hijacked plane.

Very simply put, as long as the doors of the plane were closed, it belonged to the FAA. But once the doors opened, the enforcement of federal airplane piracy law became the responsibility of the FBI. What that really means is this: once the plane lands, the FBI takes charge.

But in those days, no agency in American law enforcement was prepared to wrest control of an airplane away from an armed and determined terrorist band. The FBI didn't have the training, the manpower, or the organization for the task. Neither did any of the large metropolitan police SWAT teams.

Everybody knew that there was a glaring problem, but no one was doing anything to address it. Aircraft hijackings had been a growth industry during the 1970s, and any organization that gave it even the slightest study soon realized that it was a problem of monumental proportions. Everybody was hoping somebody else would take the lead, and it looked as if we would have to be that somebody.

During that week in the classroom, we studied every example of a Western power successfully taking a plane back from hijackers. It didn't take long. There were only two.

The French counterterrorist service, GIGN, had resolved a hijacking principally by the fires of their snipers. But a wounded hijacker had killed the commander of the force when the commander led a detachment onto the plane.

In the second instance, the German federal police CT force GSG-9, assisted by two British SAS members, had executed an assault to retake a hijacked Lufthansa 737 that had been flown to Mogadishu, Somalia, in October 1977. Although ultimately a success, the assault could easily have become catastrophic. Once in the plane, the German force got bogged down in a long gunfight. During the battle, the terrorist leader, who was in the cockpit, managed to throw two hand grenades into the passenger cabin before he was killed. Fortunately, the seats absorbed the worst of the blast and shrapnel.

In the official after-action review that the Germans shared with us, they freely admitted that they had been unprepared for the assault they had undertaken and that the plan they had put together to retake the plane was ad hoc. Though pleased they had recovered the hostages, they knew they might not be so lucky the next time. There had to be a better method of executing an aircraft assault.

Our guys went to work on the problem. By studying all the terrorist hijackings in the past decade, we determined that there were very few occasions when snipers alone could resolve a situation. But one obstacle for the snipers turned out to be smaller than anticipated.

The leader of a hijacking force usually positioned himself in the cockpit of the plane. After all, that's the control center. Often, other members of the terrorist force gravitated to the cockpit as well. If the snipers could kill any terrorists located in the cockpit when the assault was initiated, the mission's chances of success would be greatly enhanced. But there was a problem.

Most sniper units believed that a bullet fired through the extremely thick glass of an airplane cockpit would be deflected enough to cause a miss or—worse—veer off path and hit one of the airplane's crew members. The FBI and Secret Service snipers thought so too, but no one had made any practical studies of the problem until we came along.

We got a truckload of cockpit glass from many types of aircraft, mounted it in metal frames, and started shooting. Our snipers determined that there wasn't much of a problem after all. The deflection was so slight that within the confines of an airplane's cockpit it made little difference to the accuracy of the shot. They could hit and kill the terrorists and leave any crew members in the cockpit unscathed. It even turned out that any glass shattered by the bullet had the consistency of sand and presented little danger to the crew.

The assaulters were confident we could hit a grounded plane in the same fashion as we would a building: by entering simultaneously, in a violently executed rush, through every access point. If we could do that, we could be on top of the terrorists so fast that we'd be able to overwhelm and kill them before they were able to make an effective response.

But how would we get up to a plane without being seen? And how would we get in all at once? How could we divide the plane into areas of responsibility and sectors of fire? And speaking of fire, just how vulnerable was a plane to catching fire during an assault? We planned to answer those and many other questions while we were in Atlanta.

After we had pumped our visitors for all they knew, we spent the rest of the week divided into teams trying to come up with some preliminary tactics. We went out to the shooting house and worked various assault drills. It didn't take long to figure out that by simultaneously entering all the entrances of a plane, we would have some teams moving and shooting directly toward one another, or teams with their backs turned to their mates.

We soon realized that while our small twelve-row section of fuselage was great for training a single four-man team, it was far too short for multiple-team training. We needed a full-length airplane fuselage with passenger and cargo components to work on these problems. Until we could get access to the real thing, we would have to be content with chalkboard drills.

But all in all, a lot of progress was made in those few days, with every member of the tribe focusing attention on killing this mastodon. This is a good example of how operational plans were developed in Delta Force—by the men who would implement them.

Beckwith laid down the law early on. Operators would develop their own tactics and operational methods. He had chosen us because we were all experienced fighters and no one needed to tell us how to go about our business. The men on the teams would determine the *how* of a mission, and Beckwith and his subordinate commanders would provide assets and coordination. But no one would ever dictate tactics to us or tell us how to risk our own lives.

With that as a given, some of our tactics discussions became pretty heated. If someone threw an idea on the table during a skull session, he had to be ready to defend it from all sides. But this was the only way we could have gone about developing these ideas. In those early days, everything we did was plowing new ground. There were no tested approaches. And mistaken ideas would be paid for in lives—not just the lives of the hostages we were supposed to rescue, but our own.

By the close of business Thursday, we had a few preliminary plans we wanted to work on. Friday morning we loaded our bags and set out for Atlanta. Later that evening, we loaded into our vans and made the short drive from the hotel to Delta Air Lines' maintenance hangar on the back of what is now called Hartsfield-Jackson Atlanta International Airport.

I can't say enough about the good folks of Delta Air Lines and the professional hospitality they showed us. We formed a valuable relationship during that first contact, a relationship that lasted many years.

Our caretaker then and for many subsequent visits was Delta Air Lines' chief of security, Joe Stone. But the tone of the relationship was established by a senior vice president of the company when he greeted us upon our arrival at the hangar and told us we would have any and all support we needed. The reason was simple, he told us. First, it was the right thing to do; and second, it could easily be one of their planes—with their passengers and crew—we would need to rescue someday.

That was an easy statement to make, but Delta Air Lines put its money where its mouth was. During our visits, we were always given their two most senior and experienced maintenance men as technical advisors, and any plane in the hangar was at our disposal. They always had a variety of planes in the hangar, but if we wanted a particular model to rehearse on, they would make it available to us, even if they had to pull one in from another city. We worked with all the other major airlines over the years, but none of them ever showed the concern and enthusiasm for what we were trying to accomplish that Delta Air Lines did.

Maybe it had something to do with sharing a family name.

We started by learning ground operations. After all, if we had to figure out how to take back an airplane from terrorists on the ground, we needed to know the mechanics of working with them. We got to drive baggage trucks and tug motors; load and unload baggage from all types of planes; drive fuel trucks and re-fuel airplanes; and crank up and operate ground power units (GPUs), the trailer-mounted jet engines that blow air into and crank a plane's engines. Our favorite ground job of all was operating the PST (potty-sucking truck), the all-important vehicle that pumps out the toilets. (Trust me, if you are ever on a plane that's taken hostage and held for more than a day, you'll cheer the arrival of the potty truck more than the rescue team.) By learning to fill the ground positions that care for the airplanes, we became comfortable on the busy flight lines and adept at blending into the environment of an airport.

We spent several hours in the wheel, tire, and brake shop and discovered something that blew one of our theories. Shooting out a plane's tires wouldn't be much, if any, help in an assault. Not only could jet planes still taxi around with blown tires, they could even take off—they have that much power. But there was another vulnerability we found that would allow us to immobilize a plane, and that immediately went into our growing playbook.

Then we got inside the planes—all kinds of them. First the narrow bodies: 707s and DC-8s; 727s, 737s, and DC-9s. We even snagged a few Convair turboprops that were still in service. Then we tackled the wide-body planes Delta flew: the giant Boeing 747 and the Lockheed L-1011. We became familiar with their internal layouts, the locations of their emergency equipment, and areas of particular danger, such as the fuel and oxygen lines.

Aircraft doors became an obsession. We learned how to operate the doors of each plane, not just from the inside but, more importantly, from the outside. It was critical that we be able to rapidly open any door or emergency exit. We had to know how to get into any plane—in the blink of an eye— and we quickly learned how to go about it.

The next problem was what to do when we got in. In practice, we found this to be less of a problem than we had anticipated. From our point of view, the passenger compartments, cockpit, and galley areas of an airplane weren't very different from the rooms in a building, except that an airplane was absolutely crammed with people.

So tactically, we could clear a plane in almost the same manner as we approached a building. Even though the plane would be filled with hostages, by the time we entered, most of them would be hunkered down in their seats. And as we found out through experimentation, the seats of an airplane are extremely tough and offer great protection from gunfire and shrapnel. Locked cockpit and lavatory doors also proved to be no problem. We found a way to get through those as if there were no locks on them.

Next we were going to need data on all the different commercial passenger planes in the world. We would need to know how high the planes sat off the ground, how high it was to the threshold of each door, which direction the doors turned, and how to disarm the emergency slides. We had to know where the emergency lighting system switches were mounted and where the fire extinguishers were. Fortunately, that information was easy to obtain from the aircraft manufacturers and individual airlines.

That was only the beginning, but it was a good beginning. Within the next six months, we compiled the greatest database of this sort in the world, covering every commercial passenger plane in existence. We reproduced the data, illustrated with dimensional sketches, and created a small handbook we christened the Encyclopedia Aeronautica. Every Delta team had a copy.

As new airplanes came out and older planes were modified, it was a simple matter to incorporate the updates.

Airlines and airplane manufacturers were most helpful with this, and they made the new models available to us for research and training. We were caught short only once, and that was easily rectified.

We finished our session in Atlanta in good spirits. The

unit's only real deficiency now was numbers: we didn't yet have a sufficient number of operators to completely cover all the positions needed to take down a 747 or an L-1011. If our growth rate held, it would be another year before we would be large enough for that task. We just hoped that until then we wouldn't have to respond to the hijacking of a wide-body airplane.

CHAPTER**TEN**

" 'Tradecraft' is a catchall term that covers all the skills an espionage agent practices while plying his trade in the field. Dead drops,[1] brief encounters,[2] pickups,[3] load and unload signals,[4] danger and safe signals,[5] surveillance and counter-surveillance[6]—all of these things, and how you plan for them and put them into effect, are part of what constitutes tradecraft."

Our instructor today looked like a high school chemistry teacher. He wasn't. He was a veteran agent with the CIA.

"Just as fieldcraft encompasses the skills a reconnaissance[7]

[1] Dead drop/dead letter drop: a (usually) public place where a message or note can be dropped off to be picked up on the sly by another operator later on.
[2] Brief encounter: a quick meeting with another operator.
[3] Pickup: picking up another operator in some way so as not to be seen together.
[4] Load/unload signal: signal that shows a dead drop has been loaded or needs to be unloaded.
[5] Danger/safe signal: an agreed-upon signal that tells another operator that there is danger present or that the way is clear.
[6] Surveillance/countersurveillance: keeping watch over a person or place or determining whether someone else is watching you.
[7] Reconnaissance: to gather information. Slang version is "recon."

patrol employs to succeed and survive on a mission behind enemy lines, so tradecraft encompasses those skills we use to perform our job.

"But tradecraft is only a means to an end. And the end we work toward is the passage of information. Specifically, information delivery or retrieval by nontechnical means. Usually this is information in the form of a message, but sometimes it comes in the form of a person. Think of it as passing notes in class without the teacher catching on." He removed his glasses and gave the class a conspiratorial grin.

I'll bet he's had that experience, I thought, *but I'll also bet his students got away with it only if he chose to ignore it.*

Horn-rim glasses, Hush Puppies shoes, leather elbow patches on a tweed jacket, square-tailed knit tie, and a longish flattop. The man didn't look like the ace CIA field agent he was. He was also, according to Colonel Beckwith, the best agent instructor on the Farm—as insiders referred to the CIA training center at Camp Perry, Virginia.

It didn't surprise me when the man fished a pipe out of a coat pocket and puffed on it as we chatted in the hallway during break. But, did this guy ever know his business. And more than just knowing it, he could teach it—a rare thing.

The colonel had worked hard to strike some sort of deal with the CIA, and we had a close, cordial relationship with them. Two of our guys were in the CIA's new agent's course, and our OTC class was receiving instruction from the agency's star trainer.

We were bearing down on the end of OTC now, and the

two major portions of training remaining would flow smoothly into each other. Many of the principles and techniques of tradecraft overlap with those employed in executive protection or bodyguard work. In fact, some Delta operators were already working a protective detail for former president Gerald Ford.

Our snipers had been shooting and sharing training techniques with the Secret Service snipers since early winter. So when President Gerald Ford planned a ski trip, the Secret Service asked us to send them a couple of ski-qualified operators to help out. They didn't have enough agents who could ski. Skiing is a common Ranger and Special Forces skill, so most of our guys were experts on the slopes. Charlie sent along two operators, the Secret Service gave them a crash course in executive protection, and they were assigned to President Ford's detail.

The guys briefed us on their return. Their mission was to sweep the slopes in front of Mr. Ford, then let him ski past while they observed and overwatched[8] the party from above, their submachine guns slung under their ski jackets. Before a turn or a blind spot on the slope, they'd ski down past the party to clear the slope below. They would do this from the top of the slope to the bottom and then race ahead to the top of the next slope and do it all over again.

What a great job! All they had to do was clear and overwatch—none of the hard work of arranging motorcades, positioning vehicles, clearing restrooms, or worrying about the crowds in the lift lines. Soon enough, we

[8] Overwatch: to stand protective guard from a hidden position.

would all find out just how demanding, monotonous, and mundane most protection work really is. But right now, we were trying to master the basics of tradecraft.

Most of this sounds glamorous and intriguing, but in the field, the practice of espionage is plain hard work—and most of it is pretty dull work at that. But to me, it beats the heck out of being chained to a desk.

Espionage has its moments of excitement, but we weren't learning tradecraft so we could be spies. Intelligence-gathering was not a field we expected to have to plow—though as things turned out, we were wrong about that. We were learning these skills to become adept at slipping into and out of foreign territory and mounting operations in unfriendly or downright hostile nations. The first thing we learned was how to case a site[9] and write a casing report.

Let's say we're going to conduct operations in a new city. We will need to plan methods for communication via message or meeting, including dead letter drops, personal meetings,[10] brief encounters, and vehicular pickups.[11] We have to find multiple sites for all these activities, and each site has to have an alternate in case it becomes compromised. As part of this, we need to set up routes that allow us to check for anyone who may be following us and places we can use to help shake off any suspected tail.

We need sites for day use and night use, and we have to

[9] Case a site: check out a place without being seen.
[10] Personal meeting: a long meeting between operators, usually in a public place.
[11] Vehicular pickup: a pickup via car. A quick stop at a corner, for instance, where one operator slides in.

be prepared for a site being rendered useless by construction work or some other unforeseen activity. We also have to make sure no one else is using a site we have selected.

That last part is very important. All covert field agents (including criminals), regardless of their nation or government, use the same kinds of sites for their activities and the same methods of tradecraft. It's like playing baseball. No matter who you play for—America, Russia, France, Israel, or whoever—the techniques are always the same.

It's wild to start casing a site for possible use and see signs that someone else is already using the location. It's as if some other dog has already watered a fire hydrant you were eyeing.

This is especially true with dead drops because there are basically only two kinds of "load" and "unload" signals: chalk marks and thumbtacks. (And with the declining use of wooden telephone poles in large cities, the thumbtack signal has probably died out.)

If you live in Washington, D.C., or New York, look around sometimes when you're out on the street. If you see a chalk streak on a wall at about the height of a person's jacket pocket, or maybe a small piece of chalk crushed on the sidewalk near a street corner, you are probably seeing a signal left by an agent. Given the demise of the Soviet Union and the passing of the Cold War, it is amazing how much of this still goes on. If you are attuned to it, you'll see it. Our instructor told us that some sites in various world capitals were covered with chalk marks; each nation's agents used a different color of chalk. It was a terrible breach of social and professional etiquette to use someone else's color. Talk about honor among thieves.

In most cases, a good site is "ordinary." It needs to be a place that no one pays any special attention to. Obviously, it also needs to lend itself to the activity taking place and the people involved. Mostly it just needs to be a busy place with lots of people and movement—another case of the successful guerrilla swimming in the sea of the people.

In those days, one favorite place for a dead drop was a public pay phone. They could be found just about anywhere, usually in a place that made it easy to conduct counter-surveillance for the agent unloading the drop. The material to be passed would be placed in a magnetic key box, the kind found at any auto parts store. To load the drop, someone would stick the magnetic box to the underside of the pay phone's shelf while making a call or looking up a number. The box was always stuck in a predetermined spot on the shelf (left front, right rear, etc.) so that when the drop was unloaded, the agent would know exactly where to reach and wouldn't have to fumble around. The "loader" would make his "load" signal as he departed.

Why all this dancing around? Simple. To provide a cutout between people and groups. No one needs to know the identity of anyone else, especially between cells, and in the event of capture and interrogation, it helps minimize the knowledge any one operative can give up. It isn't foolproof. But it makes the work of the other side that much more difficult and time consuming, and time is a precious and perishable commodity in intelligence work.

Even the best-laid plans can become exasperatingly

fouled up. Some years later, I was in charge of the tradecraft portion of OTC. My team and I spent several weeks in Atlanta setting up sites and writing casing reports for the exercise, only to have most of our sites sealed off at the last minute because of a movie being shot downtown. It was a valuable lesson because that snag was exactly the sort of thing that could happen during an operation.

On another training session, one of our guys was supposed to follow an "agent" to a meeting site. Our guy spotted the man he thought was his target, believed he saw the "safe" and "follow me" signals, and proceeded to follow the man all over El Paso, Texas. After two hours of bus rides and mall-crawling, our guy became frustrated, stepped close to the man he'd been following, and hissed in his ear, "Buddy, don't you think it's about time we put an end to this nonsense?"

The unintentional "agent" looked at the hulking, angry stranger at his shoulder muttering what could only be a crazed and perverted threat, threw his hands in the air, and ran screaming down the street.

Fortunately for our guy, his teammates had been following along for sheer enjoyment. So they plucked their dumbstruck teammate off the street and whisked him to our safe house, where the rest of us—who had been getting constant radio updates on our "Wrong Way Ferrigan"—had gathered to complete our comrade's humiliation and sense of inadequacy.

That was funny when it happened and it's still a funny tale today. But that sort of mistake can have tragic consequences.

Years ago in Sweden, Israeli Mossad agents made a similar misidentification and assassinated a man they thought had been one of the Palestinian terrorists involved in the Munich Olympics Massacre. This sort of business is like packing parachutes—we *always* have to be sure.

Surveillance and countersurveillance were the meat of the course and had the most pertinence for us. This included finding and following a subject on foot or by vehicle, knowing when to close in tightly on him and when to give him free range, and above all, knowing how to stay invisible. To help us hone this skill, our instructor sent us on practice missions through the cities of North Carolina and Virginia.

Even in training it was a nerve-racking business. At the least, our activities could arouse the suspicion of the local police. And in our case, the police in every city we used had been alerted and were watching for us. It seemed unfair at the time, but our instructor had good reason to make the program as realistic as possible. That was what the real world would be like.

In preparation for the executive protection phase of training, we took a driving course. But not a normal driving course by any stretch of the imagination. It certainly wasn't "defensive." In fact, it was a course in "offensive" driving— in how to use a car or a convoy of cars as a weapon.

Two of our OTC instructors had been working with the State Department's Office of Diplomatic Protection and had undergone its program of instruction. From there they journeyed to Sear's Point, California, and attended Bob

Bondurant's racing school. Now they brought home what they had learned.

The Dynamic Driving Course was one of those rare things that are so much fun they never feel like work. Much like parachuting, the more difficult and dangerous the task, the more we enjoyed it. But I guess it's every man's dream come true, learning to handle a car like a stunt driver and getting paid to do it. (Years later, during the war in Panama, my colonel's young Humvee driver told me that the thing he liked most about war was that he got to drive any way he wanted and nobody could do anything about it.)

The first thing we did was go out and rent a dozen cars. Our instructors had learned the hard way that we shouldn't use our own vehicles for this sort of thing. One of our guys had rolled his own car preparing for the class, and when he asked if the unit would cover the repair cost, Beckwith said he wouldn't pay for the damage because—in the colonel's own words—"That was just stuuuuupid!"

The rental car route worked well for a year or so, until just about every rental agency within fifty miles figured out what was going on. But by the time we were finally banned by the agencies, we had put together our own training fleet.

Early one morning we took our cars and equipment to the airfield at Camp Mackall, a subpost of Fort Bragg. Since the 1950s, Mackall had been home to the first phase of Special Forces training.

It was the perfect spot for what we were doing. We could use the huge triangular airfield with its six-thousand-foot runways and adjacent taxiways as our "skidpan" and racetrack. And because it was tucked away in such a remote location, we could train to our hearts' content in peace and security.

Donald Michael Feeney was our chief instructor. Donny was an Irish-Italian street kid from Brooklyn. When I arrived for Selection, he was one of the cadre members, and when we started OTC, Donny was one of our instructors. He was as tough as a railroad spike, with alert flashing brown eyes and a keen intelligence. He was one of the most courageous men I'd ever known. You could have no better friend than Don Feeney. And no more relentless an enemy.

Out here on the skidpan, Donny was in his element: fast cars and few rules. His assistant instructor was Bill Oswalt, the cadre member who had issued my equipment when I reported in at Camp Aberdeen.

The next five days were a blur of motion and speed. Don and Bill took us through the basics of setting up a vehicle for high-performance action and then walked us through handling dynamics. We learned to feel where the weight was loaded on a car—front, rear, and sides—and how that affected braking and control. We learned how to hit the apex of a curve, use a roadway or single lane to best advantage, and bring a car to a controlled stop in less than a third of the normal distance. Next came controlled slides and reversing movements, sliding 90-degree turns left and right, the forward 180-degree turn, and the reverse 180.

Then we put it all together and chased one another around a track that had been marked around the airfield with traffic cones. We had a good turn of luck when it rained that afternoon and we were able to practice our newfound skills on a wet surface. The next day we brought out several junkers from the property disposal yard and practiced using a car as a weapon. We learned interesting little tricks such as how to spin out another vehicle, how to hit a car and bring it to an immediate halt without harming ourselves, and how to punch through a roadblock.

Most of it was a lot of fun, but as always, it was a highly competitive atmosphere. Nobody wanted to be the one who inevitably slid out of control and out of action. The only thing that gave me a rough time was when Bill had me ride with him and operate a video camera while he chased Donny around the track. By the time we were into the second circuit around the track, I was howling at Bill to stop the car.

"What's the matter?" he yelled over the noise of screaming tires.

"I'm seasick!" I yelled back. "Let me out before I puke!"

Bill pulled over to the side of the track and stopped. I climbed out, dry heaving, and wobbled around on shaky legs until I found my equilibrium again. Bill thought it was a riot until I drove the car and he tried his hand at watching a sliding, turning, braking, bouncing, accelerating world through a viewfinder. When I pulled over to let him get his color back, it was no longer such a great joke.

The last day and a half we spent on formation driving—operating within a multi-car convoy and using the vehicles as a weapon to protect the "limo." This was the heart of what we were learning: lead vehicle, limo, follow car—and how to maneuver those three vehicles as one.

We broke at lunch on Friday and got ready to depart. Before we left, Donny gave those of us who had been detailed to turn in the cars enough money to buy new tires for our rental vehicles.

"Scatter out to different tire stores in Fayetteville," he said, "and make sure you bring me back a receipt. I gotta account for that money!" He doled out twenty-dollar bills from a wad as big as his fist.

I had a little trouble with the man who put the tires on my vehicle. As soon as he realized it was a rental car, he became indignant that I was buying tires for it.

"I wouldn't pay for them tars if I wuz you, mister. The rental agency never shoulda let that car go out with 'em. Tars in that kinda condition . . . It's dangerous. You coulda been hurt." He shook his head in disgust as he looked at the bald tires with their steel belts shining through here and there.

"Dang it, I'll call 'em myself," he huffed, moving heavily to the phone. "They'll have to listen to me. Ah'm a tar per-feshunal."

"No, man, that's OK, don't worry about it." I stayed his hand on the telephone. "I'll just have them call you if they have any problems with it. Just don't worry about it."

"Well . . . awright, mister, if that's what you want." He squinted at the wad of bills I had stuffed into his hand as if it was hush money. "But it ain't right, and I wouldn't put up with it muhsef." He reluctantly gave me the receipt.

A concerned citizen, I thought as I drove back to the airport to turn in the car. It turned out I wasn't the only one to have that sort of reaction from a "tar per-feshunal."

From then on, at the end of every driving session, we replaced the tires ourselves at our own motor pool.

There are two principal methods of providing executive protection:[12] the Secret Service way—and everyone else's.

The Secret Service can and does pull out all the stops; in fact, it acts as much like the gestapo as any agency in the United States government. It has to. It is protecting the single biggest lightning rod for hostile intentions on the face of this earth. I don't envy it the task.

When protecting a president, a vice president, their families, or presidential candidates while traveling, the Secret Service calls upon—and gets—the assistance of every police force and governmental agency within the jurisdictions through which the official party travels.

The men and women of the Secret Service do a heck of a job, but without the tremendous assistance of those other host forces, the Secret Service could never provide the level of protection it gives to those in its charge.

The Secret Service is the best-dressed and -groomed group of people you have ever seen. This is an old joke, but it has some validity. If you don't know which person in a crowd is the American president, just pick out the seedy-looking man in the middle of a cluster of great-looking folks. The members of the presidential and vice-presidential details are beautiful. There's just no other way to describe them.

---

[12] Executive protection doesn't always mean protecting executives. It often means protecting a president or dignitary.

The Secret Service gave us our first lessons in what would become for Delta a very important tasking. Two senior Secret Service agents, Tommy and Francis, came from Washington to spend a few days with us and guide us through the classroom sessions of protection. The single most important thing we learned about from these men was the relationship we must maintain with our protectee, who was called the principal.

The first thing the director of the Secret Service told a newly elected president, Tommy said, was that a whole lot of people had voted against him, a whole lot of people hated him, a fair number of people wished him no good at all, and a substantial number of people would kill him if they could. Tommy said it was important to let the president know that regardless of the feeling of joy and light he got from adoring crowds of well-wishers, and despite the genuine concern the vast majority of the nation had for its president, the feeling was not universal.

Then we were given a history lesson on the attempts that had been made upon the lives of presidents and presidential candidates over the years. (The Secret Service was actually founded in 1865 to suppress counterfeit currency, but took over presidential protection responsibilities after President McKinley was assassinated in 1901.)

Next we learned the Secret Service way of providing security. Simply put, it consists of multiple concentric circles of protection placed around the principal. The outer circles perform the missions of detection and deflection of potential problems while the innermost circle "covers and evacuates" the principal in the event of an attack.

If you've watched the footage of the shooting of President Ronald Reagan, then you've seen a textbook example of what happens in that situation. At the sound of the gun going off, the agents around the president dove on him, shielded him with their bodies, shoved him into the limo, and evacuated him from the area. They were operating on trained instinct: cover him up and get him away from danger.

On the street, the agent nearest the assailant at the sound of the shot yelled, "Gun!" and grabbed both the pistol and the hand that was holding it. His focus was on taking the control of the weapon away from the attacker. The other agents, police officers, and citizens present piled on and crushed the shooter to the ground.

Most security work consists of making your principal just a little more difficult to take on than someone else in hopes of encouraging the bad guys to take their business elsewhere. The problem the Secret Service faces is that there is only one president of the United States. And someone intent on bagging a president—for reasons political or mental—usually won't settle for anyone else.

I worked with the Secret Service on only one occasion, as the counterattack team leader for Vice President Bush's detail when he visited Fort Bragg. That wasn't a particularly onerous task, since he was on what was probably some of the most secure ground in the United States.

At the end of our training, we bid Tommy and Francis a warm goodbye, full of the sincere thanks and affection we felt for those tremendous men and the service they represented. The next day, we welcomed a pair of trainers from an agency we were to have a long and close relationship with—the U.S. Department of State. This was when we learned how the rest of the world had to go about protecting a principal—with fewer people, poor-to-useless local police or other support services, and limited intelligence on any possible threats in the area.

Ambassadorial protection agents did not have the massive resources the Secret Service could call upon. In the really bad places, they had only themselves and a handful of locally recruited (and often minimally trained) bodyguards. In the event of an attack, the protective force would have to not only "cover and evacuate" but also fight their way out.

That was when Charlie Beckwith stepped in and offered them a deal they couldn't refuse.

Charlie told the State Department he would provide them with some men for posting to their most threatened embassies, men who could not only fight, but train and lead local bodyguards—something we were good at that State didn't like doing. All State had to do was provide initial training in their methods. After that, we would train our own people. And to prevent any embarrassment brought about by the idea that State had to bring in hired guns, our men would operate under Department of State cover while on assignment.

For us, it meant a permanent position in some really bad places in the world—places where we would probably have to operate in the near future. It gave us contacts in an agency that had a very real and strong impact on our potential operations, and it allowed us to start building trust with them. It would pay off for us time after time in the years to come.

Our two new guests, Alton and Raymond, painted a bleak picture as they briefed us on what we were faced with around the world. Then we dove into the subject at hand: how to protect an ambassador of the United States of America in a place where so many people were determined to kill him.

Avoiding situations and places that can become problems is the name of the game. If we are doing our job well, the boss will argue with us now and again about being overly cautious. But that's OK. It's better than sitting in front of a congressional panel explaining how we managed to let the representative of the American people in a foreign country be killed while he or she was entrusted to our care. To this day, no member of Delta Force has ever had to do that.

Now it was time to practice what we thought we knew.

For a few days, Alton and Raymond took turns being the principal and the detail leader as we rehearsed our skills around Fayetteville and Raleigh. Then we started rotating in as detail leader, while one of the instructors provided a running critique and threw problems at us. Something as simple as a flat tire on the limo on the way to an appointment in another city could throw a whole day out of kilter.

As we became proficient at handling the smaller, mundane problems, our teachers would hit us with the big ones:

The principal is at a dinner party in a private residence when the house is hit by rockets and catches fire and there is small arms fire in the street outside.

195

An irate local national tries to assault the principal at a press conference in a hotel lobby.

A local police checkpoint tries to stop the principal's motorcade at gunpoint.

The principal's wife wants you to send the detail's local bodyguards to pick up her friends for an official tea party she's hosting at the embassy. She thinks it would be a nice touch.

The principal suffers a heart attack at a diplomatic dinner.

Each one of these situations happened without notice, and it taught us a tremendous lesson. *Always expect something bad to happen and be ready to act.*

I was the detail leader when the principal had his "heart attack" at the dinner party. It's pretty disconcerting to look calmly around the room and then back at your protectee just in time to see him drop face-first into his soup as the room erupts into turmoil.

One of the most trying aspects of the job is that it's difficult to take care of the physical needs of ourselves and our staffs. Just getting a chance to go to the bathroom can be a trying experience. And something as simple as getting everyone fed at mealtimes takes careful planning. If the principal takes thirty minutes for a meal, that means we can feed only a few of our people during that time and we have to make arrangements for the others before and after normal mealtimes. It is the rare protectee who realizes, much less cares, about something as simple as making sure the people protecting his life have time to eat.

The work is mentally demanding, not because of an intellectual challenge, but because it requires unrelenting vigilance and attention to detail. We are *never* able to relax, and that translates into physical fatigue, making it imperative that we maintain some sort of physical conditioning program. And that, too, has to be worked in around the principal's daily schedule. Because like the basic training drill sergeant, "You get 'em up in the morning, you put 'em to bed at night, you're with 'em their every waking hour—and some nights while they sleep."

Once our instructors were happy with our local performance, we took our show on the road to Washington, D.C. It was much more comfortable doing that sort of thing in Washington than it ever was in Fayetteville. A three-car motorcade in D.C. is part of the natural scenery, but in North Carolina, it was like the circus band coming down Main Street.

In Washington the presence of a full-blown protective detail was so common that few people paid us any attention and we were able to concentrate on our work. And besides, Washington wasn't just *a* world capital; it was *the* world capital. So if we could do a professional job there, under the scrutiny of the best protective agencies on the planet, we should have no problems operating anywhere in the world.

Things went so smoothly that it turned out to be a pretty dull exercise. In order for us to rotate everyone through the various positions on the detail, we broke into two groups and alternated working day and night shifts.

We spent a few busy days and nights in Washington under the careful eye of the State Department security hierarchy and then quietly concluded our training with those very capable people.

After the out-briefing with our trainers, Donny and Bill told us to wait for them in the hotel until they got back. They would have some instructions for us when they returned from exchanging the official thank-yous and farewells at the State Department.

Something's cooking, I thought as we maneuvered through traffic. This bit about "stand by for instructions to follow" had a whiff of Selection to it. Well, we'd already started saying "Selection is a never-ending process."

And no matter what, OTC was just about over and we would be forming into teams soon—which didn't mean there weren't still a few surprises yet to come.

CHAPTER**ELEVEN**

Gerhard Altmann was born in Germany. When just a boy of fifteen, he had been issued an ill-fitting uniform and a Panzerfaust antitank rocket launcher and sent into the rubble-filled streets of the dying city of Berlin to battle the omnivorous Red Army during Hitler's Third Reich.

Captured by the Russians after twelve days of unspeakably brutal fighting, the young Gerhard was interned in a prisoner of war camp for several weeks until he and a number of other boy soldiers were able to make an escape. He survived that terrible postwar winter by the sheer toughness of youth. Later that year he was turned in by an informer for scavenging machine guns and was interned once again. He escaped once more, but this time, he made his way to Munich, where he found work with the U.S. Army as a laborer in a military warehouse. He worked at night and finished school during the day.

Two years later, with the assistance of some of his new American friends, Gerhard left for the United States, where he promptly enlisted in the army and was almost immediately sent to fight at the outbreak of war on the Korean Peninsula.

Following the war, Altmann completed a university degree under the GI Bill, and he returned to the army just in time to become one of the earliest members of the army's newly formed Special Forces, where he met Charlie Beckwith during a tour in Vietnam. He must have made quite an impression on the future commander of First Special Forces Operational Detachment–Delta, because Beckwith selected him to be one of the original staff officers when the unit was born.

On Friday afternoons back at the Ranch, Altmann delivered a worldwide intelligence update to the assembled membership of Delta Force. Now we were assembled in a large suite in our Washington hotel, and Major Altmann was briefing us on the final phase of the Operator Training Course, appropriately termed the Culmination Exercise.

"My young friends," said Altmann, striking a Mussolini pose complete with a lifted chin, "you have come far, very far indeed, and now you must demonstrate that you can apply the skills you have acquired by your persistence, diligence, and hard work. The task before you is not easy. And why should it be? The simple truth is that our mission is not easy. Were it otherwise, we would not be here now, for other men would have already shouldered the burden you now so nobly carry."

He dropped the Mussolini act and continued in a normal voice.

"This is your final exam, and I believe it to be one that will test your abilities to the fullest. I like to think of this as an exercise in resourcefulness, and before you are finished, I believe you will think of it that way too."

He pointed toward the back of the room.

"On that table there is a folder for each of you, marked with your code names. Inside you will find one thousand dollars in cash and a set of instructions. You will find an emergency contact phone number on the inside cover of the folder. Use that number only in the event of an emergency that requires you to come out of the play of the exercise. In all other situations, you are to rely on your designated covers for status and action. You do not have authority to break any national, state, or local laws. However, you may treat regulations according to your own discretion." He smiled in punctuation to that last remark.

"And, oh, by the way"—he slapped his forehead with the heel of his hand—"I almost forgot. The FBI starts looking for you in about three hours." He lifted a wrist and consulted his watch. "Or less. They seem to be laboring under the misconception that you are foreign agents of one flavor or another. I think it would be very unpleasant for you to be apprehended and interrogated by those most diligent and persuasive gentlemen.

"And since there are no questions—and I know that each of you has a pressing and diversified itinerary—my wish is that you all . . . have a good 'un."

He dismissed us with a flourish of the hand like a master of ceremonies gesturing for the start of a show.

Three hours, I thought, *before the hounds hit the trail with the smell of our blood under their noses.* I located my folder, counted the money inside, and signed for the package on the roster nearby. *Man, I've got to get cracking. But not in such a hurry that I start making mistakes. First I'll go back to my room, read my instructions, and make a plan that will get me through the next twenty-four hours.*

I left the briefing suite and ambled down the corridor to the elevator bank.

Guys are already behaving in character, I thought as I waited for the elevator. The more excitable ones had taken off like quail flushed from a covey, but most of the men simply moved off as if they were winding up an ordinary, boring day.

My method of preparing myself for the ordeal ahead was to make haste slowly. To purposefully slow my movements and thoughts—at least until the adrenaline rush was over. That was how I had learned to impose self-discipline and keep from running off half-cocked.

Back in my hotel room, I stashed the money and sat down to read my instructions. They directed me to a personal meeting and read as follows:

Personal Meeting Plan
1. *Purpose:* Conduct personal meeting with local agent
2. *Date/Time:* 9 June 1979, 2200 hours
3. *General Location:* The Embassy Row Hotel, 2015 Massachusetts Ave. NW, Washington, D.C. (See area map.)
4. *Specific Location:* Embassy Lounge on the 1st floor, adjacent to the "Le Consulat" Restaurant
5. *Contact Procedures:*

a. Enter lounge, spot agent, and join him at table or bar.

b. Agent will give brief verbal instructions about recontact and pass written mission instructions by placing them inside newspaper or magazine, which he will leave on the table upon departure.

c. Team Member will retrieve the newspaper/ magazine and depart a suitable time later.

6. *Recognition Signals* (Bona Fides):

a. Visual: Both Team Member and Contact Agent will make visible one (1) red and one (1) black felt-tip pen.

b. Verbal: Team Member: "Have you been waiting long? We got hung up in traffic."
Contact: "No, not too long. The traffic does get bad sometimes."

7. *Danger Signal:* Team Member or Agent, upon recognizing danger or compromise, will scratch side of the nose with finger.

8. *Cover:* Embassy Lounge was recommended as a place to visit when in Washington, D.C.

9. *Security Considerations:* The Embassy Row Hotel is used by foreign dignitaries. Real agents are likely to be throughout the hotel. Smooth civilian clothing is most appropriate.

10. *Alternate Contact:* If scheduled meeting does not take place within ten minutes of time specified, or if meeting has to be terminated prematurely, attempt to reestablish contact exactly two (2) hours later at the same point.

11. *Instructions to Ensure Continuity:* If neither the scheduled nor the alternate meetings take place, attempt to make contact by calling telephone number *202-324-2805.* Identify yourself as *"Mr. Jones"* and ask when and where you could meet with *"Mr. Alden."*

12. *Props Required:* Contact Agent: Newspaper or magazine and red and black felt-tip pens

Team Member: Red and black felt-tip pens

The last page of instructions consisted of an area map showing the street location of the hotel and a sketch of the hotel layout depicting the locations of the restaurant, the lounge, and the hotel's main entrance.

After reading the meeting instructions, I called the front desk and extended my stay for two days. I knew that the FBI would start at the hotel, and I wanted to keep their attention focused there for at least one night. Then I got out the Yellow Pages and looked up the numbers of several van rental companies. I wrote the numbers down on a scrap of paper from my wallet instead of the pad from the nightstand—no need to leave behind any impressions of those phone numbers.

Then I went to the "Hotel" section in the Yellow Pages and copied the numbers of six D.C.-area hotels to the phone pad. I called each number and inquired about room availability and price. When I finished, I pulled the page with the numbers off the phone pad, tore it into small pieces, and threw them in the wastebasket. All I wanted to do was leave just enough evidence of a trail to slow down any trackers. By the next day, I would have put some distance between where they were looking and where I was. I needed to trade space for time.

I checked the room to make sure I hadn't left anything behind that I didn't intend to leave and made my way out of the building. I was traveling light, with only a small suitcase and a suit bag, so luggage was not a burden. I walked a few blocks from the hotel, hailed a cab, and told the driver to take me to the train station. As soon as we pulled up to the station entrance, I paid the driver, told him to keep the change, and hopped out.

I walked inside the station, wandered through the building, and came back out again through a side entrance, where I caught a cab to the Greyhound bus station. I knew that Gerhard had said we had a three-hour window of grace before the hunt started, but I didn't believe it and felt it was better to get with the program right away.

At the bus station, I changed clothes and stashed my luggage in a locker. I wouldn't leave it there very long, but I didn't want it with me for a while. At a pay phone outside, I called the van rental companies whose numbers I had written down in the hotel and selected the one that seemed to be the smallest company of all, one not affiliated with any national chain.

"Yes sir, that's right," I said to the manager. "Just a decent cargo van I can use to move to my new apartment. No, I don't have anything really heavy, mostly just my clothes and some other personal things. I don't have much in the way of furniture. Biggest thing I own is a television set and a bag of golf clubs. What's that? OK, that's just what I need and the price is good. I'll be there by two o'clock. Thank you, sir; see you then."

With transportation taken care of, I decided to have a bite of lunch and do some planning. I thought about the rest of the day while I had a sandwich at a small diner near the bus station. *No need to make any plans for tomorrow because more than likely, I'll be responding to whatever instructions I receive at the meeting tonight.* For now I just needed to make the most of the time I had until the meeting at ten o'clock that night. I finished my sandwich and went to collect my van.

The vehicle was just about perfect. Seven years old, no side or rear windows, cream colored with a few dents and scrapes here and there. Yep, it'd do just fine. I left a cash deposit instead of using a credit card and drove off to find a Kmart.

It didn't take long to find one. I bought just a few things I had calculated I would require: a sleeping bag and a patio lounge-chair cushion, an assortment of pens, a couple of notepads, a box of white chalk and a box of colored chalk, a small leather-covered address book, a pair of dark blue coveralls, a couple of baseball caps, a small pair of cheap binoculars, a Styrofoam cooler, a towel and a couple of washcloths, a roll of duct tape, a set of maps of D.C., Maryland, and Virginia, and a small toy water pistol.

Next stop was a grocery store, where I picked up fruit, canned goods, saltine crackers, several jugs of water, and a bottle of household ammonia. Then I drove around to the back of the store and found the last items I needed at the Dumpsters: a couple of cardboard boxes to hold my "goods" and a five-gallon plastic bucket with a lid to serve as a toilet.

Then I drove two blocks away to another parking lot, where I packed and rearranged my things in the van and filled the water pistol with ammonia. To prevent it from leaking, I sealed the tip of its nozzle with a Band-Aid from my wallet.

Now I was set. I could live in the van for an extended period if necessary, and if I had to go underground for a few days, I could safely hole up somewhere without having to come up for air. I had a means of self-protection, just in case of emergencies. The water pistol full of ammonia was a trick I'd learned from an old man I'd worked with as a young boy on a delivery truck. It would stop a vicious dog in its tracks and worked equally well on people, but it wouldn't cause lasting harm. And just as important, it wasn't a firearm, which would be about useless in this situation and could only serve to get me in trouble if a cop got a glimpse of it. But there was nothing wrong with a harmless water pistol.

When I was happy with my arrangements, I drove into town to have a look at the area around the hotel where the meeting would take place. I wanted to get a feel for the streets and traffic routing as well as find some easy-to-recognize landmarks on all four sides of the hotel. I chose several different options for places to park and ran getaway routes from them. I wanted to have several different ways to get completely out of the area as rapidly as possible or to make a short run and dodge into some hiding spot.

After I had run the routes in the van, I went back

and parked in each spot and walked around the areas to make sure I knew what the ground looked and felt like when approached from different directions. I also found and noted on my mental map several spots I could duck into and elude a pursuer. I was pretty confident that if it came to a footrace, I could outdistance any FBI agent. But that would be only to lay a false trail and then get back to the van.

When I felt that I knew the area like it was my own neighborhood, I went back to the van and drove out to a marina on the Potomac River near National Airport. I spoke with the man running the fuel dock and told him I was there to meet my boss who was bringing his boat up from Virginia Beach. Boats are a passion of mine, so that gave me a cover for status that allowed me to be in the area without drawing much attention.

I could hang out in the lounge, use the showers, walk around the docks, and generally blend into the scenery. Marinas have people coming and going at all hours, but they are also abnormally crime free, and consequently, cops and other investigative types seldom, if ever, venture into them.

In fact, whenever I've had occasion over the years to slip into and out of various "interesting" spots in the world, I've preferred to do so by boat. It's like wearing a cloak of invisibility. A person can come and go undetected and un-molested. Bus stations, train terminals, and airports are all crawling with surveillance, but the waterfront goes unob-served.

I had dinner in the marina restaurant, watched the

evening news in the lounge, and showered. Back in the van, I changed into a dark blue suit and a pair of comfortable shoes I could run in if necessary. Then I made a mental review of where I was going and what *should* happen there while I placed one red-tipped and one black-tipped felt pen in the outer pocket of my new address book. When everything was ready, I sat for a few minutes to make sure I was master of myself and prepared for action.

My contact was the last person in the world I would have expected—which proved the wisdom of my own adage to expect the unexpected.

He was an exquisitely dressed man in his sixties, with a head full of elaborately coifed silver hair, and he was as drunk as a lord. He had the appropriate colored pens displayed, a red one tucked behind his left ear, a black one behind his right, and he was haranguing the bartender, who was doing his best to keep his distance. I slid onto the stool next to the guy, ordered a drink, and put my address book holding the colored pens on the bar between us.

After a few seconds, he felt my presence and turned in my direction. He squinted at me through a boozy fog and started to say something. Then he noticed the address book with the pens showing, gulped like a fish, stared at the pens for a minute longer as the cogs rumbled in his befuddled mind, and then looked up at me with a conspiratorial grin splattered across his face.

"Hey! It's my buddy! How ya doin', buddy?" he slurred at me as he swiveled perilously around on his stool.

"I'm OK," I replied. "Have you been waiting long? We got hung up in traffic."

"Nah, I ain't been waitin' long—I ain't been waitin' long at all. But the traffic—the traffic"—he belched—"the traffic does get pretty bad sometimes, don't it?" He gave me a leering wink and smiled hugely in self-satisfaction at getting the phrase right.

"You a Yankees fan, ain't you?" he suddenly yelled. "You seen what those nitwits did in Chicago yesterday?" He waved a folded newspaper in my face. "It's right here in the paper. Look for ya'self. Jus' take a look at it, 'cause I don't even want to think about it no more. It's . . . it's . . . it's . . . jus'—terrible!" He put his head down on his folded arms, and I swear to God, he started weeping.

I put my address book on top of the paper he had given me and then awkwardly patted the lunatic on the back while he rolled his head back and forth in the crook of his arms, sobbing and wailing as if the world was coming to an end. I could feel every eye in the lounge locked on us as I looked around in embarrassment. The people at the bar and nearby tables had given us a clear circle with a diameter of at least ten feet. It was as if we were known carriers of bubonic plague. I felt like I was in a bad dream, one of those in which you suddenly realize you're standing naked in a crowded room. It was surreal, but I was trapped and would have to extricate myself as best as possible from an awkward and uncomfortable situation.

So much for a subtle and low-key contact.

"Hey, man, it's OK. They just had a bad day. They'll do better; I'm sure they will. You can't keep the ol' Yankees down," I said as I gripped him by the upper arm and rubbed his back as though I was consoling a child grieving over a broken toy. "They just had a bad day was all. It happens to every team."

"You really think so?" he asked as he raised his head, gave me a hopeful look, and wiped the tears from his swollen eyes.

"Yeah, of course they will. Here." I handed him a paper napkin and motioned for him to wipe the snot from his upper lip.

"Well, in that case, what say we have another drink!" he yelled as happiness shot across his face, clearing away the misery of his former anguish and woe.

"Why not?" I said, gesturing to the bartender to give us a refill. He glanced at my partner, then gave me a raised eyebrow. When I silently mouthed, "It's OK," he shrugged in exculpation and turned to make the drinks.

"Hey, look, buddy, I've got to make a trip to the men's room. You'll be OK till I get back, won't you?" I asked as I slid the newspaper and address book under my arm.

"Sure, I'll be OK; take your time. But just remember," he shouted at me across the lounge as I walked away, "wash your hands like your mama taught you!" He started to laugh at his sophomoric joke, but instead, he collapsed into a choking, coughing fit that bent his head back to his folded arms on the bar, where he heaved and hacked and gasped for air as if he was in the throes of congestive heart failure.

It took every atom of restraint and self-discipline I could muster to keep from breaking into a one-man stampede as I strolled through the lounge toward the men's room. *Man,* I thought as I turned a corner, *was that for real?*

211

If it hadn't been, then it was without doubt the best acting job I'd ever witnessed, and I'd seen some good ones during my years as a platoon sergeant. I went past the men's room, down the next corridor, and out the nearest exit. Time to make tracks.

I made an abrupt departure for a couple of reasons. One, we were drawing too much attention (which I could only believe was purposeful), and two, I wanted to start checking for surveillance right away. By making a sudden exit, I thought I might force a surveillance team to show itself. Once outside, I walked rapidly away from the hotel and across a side street. When a raft of traffic clogged the avenue, I jaywalked through the cars and doubled back on the other side. That would jam up any vehicle following me on the street and would make a foot detail either walk on by me or scramble around a couple of corners to get back in formation. If I saw anyone on the street reverse himself or herself when I did the crossover, I intended to break into a run.

None of that happened, so I continued zigzagging around for a while. I circled the block on which I had parked the van, walked ten meters past it, and then spun about and made a beeline back to the van. I didn't see anyone behind me on either side of the street as I jumped in, cranked up, and pulled away.

There wasn't another vehicle on the street as I drove off, but that didn't mean a lot. If I was the target of surveillance, a good team would have me bracketed on parallel streets and catch me at a corner. I made a couple of turns and timed two stop lights in succession so that I punched through the intersections mid-yellow. I checked the rearview mirror to see if anybody had followed me through. Looked like my "six"[1] was clear, so I headed back across the Potomac River as directly and quickly as possible.

I cruised toward Fort Myer and pulled into the back lot of a hotel across from the fort's main entrance. I changed out of my suit and into jeans, sweatshirt, running shoes, and baseball cap. Now I was back in the guise of a normal working-class guy. Once I changed my costume, I turned on the van's lights, wedged down the brake pedal with a tire iron, and climbed out to check the vehicle. The best way to make a vehicle easy to follow at night is to punch a small hole in a taillight. That lets a small spot of white light shine in the middle of the red lens, making the vehicle stand out from all the others. It's a simple trick, but extremely effective.

I was in luck—no holes. I checked all the lights and the blinkers; I didn't want a cop stopping me for a burned-out light. Next I took my flashlight and checked all around and under the van, especially on the sides. At the marina I had purposefully driven through several mudholes to throw a nice layer of muddy water and dirt on the sides of the van and underneath the chassis. Anybody screwing with the van would wind up smearing or scuffing that faint dirt layer. No signs of that, either.

I knew there was only a small chance I would already have been targeted. The FBI would have a limited number

---

[1] Six: the "six o'clock position"—your rear.

of agents they could throw into a training exercise such as this. And more than twenty of us wandering around Washington like tadpoles in a pond would make life difficult for even a large surveillance operation. But a healthy dose of paranoia wasn't necessarily a bad thing, and I didn't want to be apprehended and blow the final exercise.

I was satisfied that no one had tampered with my vehicle and that I hadn't been followed to this location. And as long as I had freedom of movement, I didn't think anyone could latch on to me. The danger areas where things could start to go bad were those choke points—the specific places I had to go—such as that last meeting. Those were the spots where a would-be tail could fall in behind me, or where I could be nabbed. When someone sets up an ambush, that spot is known as the Kill Zone. I was determined to head into those dangerous places with all the caution of a crippled antelope limping past a pride of lions.

Back in the van, I pulled a manila envelope from the folds of the newspaper I had received from my drunken contact and read the contents. An index card clipped to a few sheets of paper read:

Mission: Unload Dead Letter Drop
(See attached Casing Report.)

I put the card back in the envelope and looked at the other papers:

Casing Report
(Dead Letter Drop)

1. *Location:* Richmond, Virginia

2. *Description of area:* Inner-city area frequented by people from all walks of life

3. *Drop Site:* Middle telephone booth (#648-9587) in a bank of five in left rear of lobby of Hotel Jefferson, 112 West Main Street (See sketch 2.)

4. *Specific Drop Location:* Underneath metal shelf inside booth (See sketch 1.)

5. *Size and Type of Container:* Magnetic key box attached to underside of shelf

6. *Servicing Time:* Between 0800 and 2200 hours only

7. Cover: Making telephone call

8. Route: When unloading, first check *Load Signal Site* (see sketch 2), park vehicle and enter lobby of *Jefferson Hotel* through main entrance. Service drop, exit, and place Unload Signal. (See sketch 2.) Depart at your discretion.

9. *Seasonal Limitations:* None

10. *Security Considerations:* Avoid loitering in the lobby. Avoid using drop between 2200 and 0800 hours.

11. *Props Required:* Loader: Magnetic key box and white chalk. Unloader: White chalk.

12. *Date of Casing:* 14 May 1979

13. *Cased by:* Eagle

14. *Load Signal:* Small piece of white chalk crushed on sidewalk in front of main entrance

(south) to *Jefferson Hotel* on *Main Street* (See sketch 2.)

15. *Unload Signal:* Small piece of white chalk crushed on sidewalk in front of side entrance (west) to *Jefferson Hotel* (See sketch 2.)

The next page of the instructions included an area map of downtown Richmond and two sketches, one showing where the magnetic box was located on the telephone shelf, the other showing a diagram of the hotel layout and the adjacent streets.

The next morning I drove past the Jefferson Hotel at 0930 hours. Sure enough, there was the load signal right out in front of the main entrance to the hotel, a half-dollar-sized splatter of white chalk crushed on the sidewalk. I found a good place to park a few blocks away, snugged up my tie, slipped on my blazer, and made my way through the river of the people going about their lives that beautiful morning.

I said good morning to several elderly couples in the lobby as I made my way to the rest room for a quick stop. I dragged out my visit a little longer than necessary to see if anyone would lose patience and come in after me, then popped back out and crossed unobserved to the bank of phones on the opposite wall.

I dropped a quarter into the phone slot and dialed an automated number that gave the correct time. While leaning closely into the small phone cubicle, I slipped my free hand under the stainless steel shelf, palmed the magnetic box that was right where the diagram had indicated it would be, and slipped it into a jacket pocket. I said thanks to the recorded voice that was still counting off the minutes, hung up the phone, and made my way to the Jefferson Street exit.

While walking back through the hotel lobby, I took a piece of chalk half the size of the last joint of my little finger from a jacket pocket and transferred it to the pocket of my slacks. I held it in my hand as I walked along. Outside the hotel, I stopped on the sidewalk directly in front of the door and quickly looked both ways up and down the sidewalk as if I was momentarily unsure about which direction to take.

In that little instant of seeming indecision, I dropped the chalk through a hole in my pocket that I had made that morning, felt it rattle its way down my leg, and glanced down long enough to note the little white lump on the sidewalk next to my shoe. Then, pretending that I had made up my mind about direction, I put my foot on the chalk and spun on it as I turned to head down the street. Leaving the unload signal had taken every bit of two or three seconds. I jaywalked to the other side of the street, turned the next corner, took a roundabout route back to the van, and ran a few countersurveillance moves as I drove out of the area. So far, so good.

A few miles away, I pulled into the parking lot of a small restaurant, where I unfolded and read the three sheets of onionskin paper that were in the magnetic box (or magic box, as I often thought of it). The first page was a directive to survey a site for 1. a vehicular pickup, and 2. a dead letter drop and write the casing reports for each site. The rest of the material was instructions for a personal meeting at 1500 hours that afternoon at the Iwo Jima, the Marine Corps War Memorial in Arlington, Virginia. At that meeting, I was to turn over my casing reports and receive additional information from my contact. We were to pass the material in a rolled newspaper or magazine. All very normal, but I would have to work fast if I was going to survey two sites, write the reports, and get back to Arlington by 1500 hours. I jumped to it.

My contact turned out to be Major Altmann himself. He was sitting on a bench, looking for all the world like a veteran lost in the contemplation of the memorial depicting that small band of heroic marines raising the American colors on the summit of Mount Suribachi. I quietly took a seat beside him, and after a few moments of my own silent contemplation, we spoke as two strangers would and then went through the formalities of exchanging the recognition sentences—the verbal equivalent of a secret handshake.

"Let us walk as we converse," said Altmann. We rose to our feet, and as we started to stroll, he put his arm through mine, as is the fashion among friends in Eastern Europe and the Middle East. It was a nice touch. Not only because it's a custom I enjoy, but because in those days the Iwo Jima Monument was known as a meeting place for gay men. Remember, in tradecraft, cover is everything.

"I must say that my friend in the bar the other night was most distressed by your abrupt departure. He wishes me to tell you he hopes he did or said nothing to cause you embarrassment," said Altmann. "However, that technique for making your exit was very effective. It was so sudden and unexpected that the FBI's surveillance team was unable to keep pace, and you had completely eluded them by the time you were on the street."

He chuckled at the pleasure of the memory.

So my gut feeling had been correct: there had been surveillance of the meeting that night.

I wanted to ask if the contact had actually been drunk or if it had been an act, but I kept silent. I preferred not knowing for certain. Some things in life just feel better when they are left as mysteries.

As we walked arm in arm, Gerhard held a rolled magazine in his free hand and occasionally used it to gesture toward the monument as though he was a historian giving a personally guided tour to a younger protégé.

"It has given me a great deal of satisfaction," he continued, "that not one of your comrades has yet been caught by the team the FBI has assembled to run you to ground. In fact, I suspect the team leader is making excuses to his superior, even as we speak, as to why he has been so conspicuously unsuccessful in the effort. This has a special appeal to me after having listened to his arrogant—and, I should add, insolent—opinion that it would be an elementary task to round up amateur practitioners of the art. I am certain your tradecraft instructor will be pleased by the results so far."

As he flourished his hand skyward for emphasis, he stumbled ever so slightly and dropped the magazine he was holding.

"Let me get that," I said. As I bent to retrieve the magazine from the ground at our feet, I exchanged it for the one I had been carrying.

"Thank you, my friend. Your young spine is more supple than the one I must contend with at this time of my life." He inclined his head in appreciation as he took the magazine I proffered. He stopped after another step or two and turned to face me.

"Do be alert," he said, looking into my face with twinkling eyes that had seen so much of the dark side of life. "The tempo of the operation is going to increase. You and your comrades will be gathering into cells, which makes for a greater chance of compromise. And though this exercise began with feelings of mutual affinity, I fear that due to their lack of success, the FBI may now take this as a personal confrontation. Therefore, if you should find yourself in a situation where physical force is used against you, I believe you would be justified in responding in kind."

He was smiling at the thought of that eventuality as we shook hands and departed for our separate destinations.

The instructions I found in the magazine directed me to conduct a vehicular pickup of a subject at the Washington mansion at Mount Vernon. I would find him in the visitors' parking lot just as the facility closed for the day. The contact would be someone I knew.

I cruised through the lot just as a stream of cars and buses was pulling out. I didn't see anyone familiar. But just as I had almost completed a circuit of the parking area, I saw a tall figure with a shock of long red hair dart from behind a small outbuilding into an edge of the parking lot where he was screened by a hedge of boxwoods.

It was John Yancy, and his timing was perfect. His path

intercepted the edge of the pavement just as I rolled up. I stopped the van for a split second while John jumped in, and then we were on the move and headed for the exit. It was a smooth and natural looking pickup that would have been difficult to observe.

I had felt neither interest in our passage nor a tail, either going in or coming out, but that meant little. So on the way back to town, we made a few "shakes and scratches" just to see if any fleas fell off.

One of the best ways to do that was to cruise into a cul-de-sac in a residential neighborhood and see who followed us in. If it was a tail, they were "burned." This meant that we knew what they looked like—along with what car they were using—so they'd have to be pulled from the surveillance team, which made life a little more difficult for the "trackers" and might cause them to make other mistakes. But we were clean.

John and I first met and hit it off during Selection. He had been a renowned recon man with Special Forces in Vietnam and was considered one of the best men to be beside during a fight. He was absolutely unflappable no matter how bad things got.

John was another of our comrades who would leave us too early. He was shot and killed just a few years later, only two weeks before he was to leave the unit for a "safer" assignment.

We compared notes as we rode along. John, too, had been servicing dead drops, casing various sites, and writing reports. In fact, he had unloaded a drop at Mount Vernon directing us to a pickup in Georgetown that evening. But first we retrieved John's gear from the flea-bitten motel where he had stashed it, and then we cruised Georgetown to ready ourselves for the pickup.

We plucked Pete Vandervoort from a bus stop just as he'd walked up and set his bags down by the bench. He was in such a hurry to get in the van that John had to remind him that it would probably be a good idea to bring his bags along for the ride. Pete agreed and jumped back out to grab his bags and give them a toss into the back of the van.

Pete was carrying information that pertained to all three of us. We would form a cell tasked with performing several collective tasks. He gave us the highlights and caught us up on his recent activities as we drove out of the city to a motel that John and I had already earmarked for our base of operations. We needed a more "normal" place to hole up. Three men living out of a van were sure to attract attention we didn't want and couldn't afford. We took two adjoining rooms at the motel and settled in to study the papers Pete had retrieved from the dead drop he had serviced just before we'd picked him up.

We were charged with several missions—complicated missions—with the potential for hazard and compromise.

We were directed to get a roster of the cleaning personnel at the U.S. Naval Observatory, a list of the number and types of weapons at a specific National Guard armory, and a copy of the next month's operations schedule from Andrews Air Force Base.

We had two days to accomplish the assignments and prepare a detailed after-action report. The material, the reports, and two passport photos of each of us were to be turned over to a contact at a personal meeting. We would get the details of that meeting from a dead drop. The instructions for servicing the drop were on the last page.

All well and good, but first we needed some nourishment and a plan. Pete folded up the sheets of paper and shoved them down the front of his pants. Unless he was strip-searched, they were undetectable and perfectly safe. Then we set out in search of a Korean restaurant. For some inexplicable reason, all three of us had a yen for kimchi that evening.

Over dinner we talked "man talk." Sports, fishing, hunting, women, politics—anything other than what we were doing. By now, the custom of watching what we said and where we said it had become such a habit that the only time we discussed "business" in an open setting was in the sanctuary of the Ranch.

Back at the motel, we determined a course of action. We would have to divide and conquer. Time was short, the tasks were tricky, and cover for action was going to be critical with a capital C. If even two of us showed ourselves at any one place, it would only cause problems. We decided to draw straws for the missions. John drew the Naval Observatory, Pete got the National Guard armory, and I received Andrews Air Force Base.

We were each going to need wheels. I figured that my van had reached the end of its useful life; if it wasn't burned (identified as being mine) yet, it would be soon, so it was time to turn it in. John scouted the Yellow Pages for several Rent-A-Wreck places and a passport photo shop while Pete and I kicked around covers for status and action.

The next morning, I dropped the guys off at two different lots to pick up cars and I drove back to turn in my van. It deserved a good rest. It had given me good service.

Pete picked me up on the street two blocks away and took me to a lot where I rented a Ford Maverick. It was the best vehicle they had on the lot—which should tell you a lot about the place. Still, the little car was a V-8 with lots of power left, and it was relatively nondescript.

Before setting off on our individual tasks, we rendezvoused in a grocery parking lot and piled in one car to a little photography shop to have the passport photos taken.

It took every hour of those two days to accomplish our assigned tasks. The methods we used were simple, didn't require elaborate covers, and could be easily imitated by someone with sinister designs—especially in those years before September 11.

John was able to obtain the roster of the people who worked on the housekeeping staff of the Naval Observatory. He also got their work histories, their addresses, and their home phone numbers.

I was able to gain the operations schedule for Andrews Air Force Base—and as a serendipitous bonus, the maintenance schedule for Air Force One for the rest of the year.

Pete made quite a haul. He not only got a copy of the weapons roster from the National Guard armory, but also found out that the bolts for the M16s were stored in the unit safe, that four bayonets were missing, and that none of the organization's M60 machine guns would work. Pete had made such a strong impression on the unit commander that he returned with an autographed picture of the two of them shaking hands and an invitation to the armory for their next weekend drill. I would have liked to be a fly on the wall to hear the tale Pete told that commander.

That afternoon, we sat down in my motel room to go over everything we had acquired and put all the material into a reportable format. Later, John went out to unload a dead drop while Pete and I worked on a draft of the report. He came back with instructions as to how we would turn over our material and a directive to case two more dead drop sites and a location for a personal meeting for the next morning. We decided that I would work on the report while my partners went out to case the sites.

I was still working on the report when they returned. We reviewed it, and once we were satisfied with everything, I made a tight bundle of the papers and went out to load a drop message confirming what we'd accomplished. Then we settled in for some sleep.

Pete went to the personal meeting at 0400 hours the next morning to turn over our report while John and I pulled countersurveillance and overwatched him just in case things got sticky. The meeting went off all right, but Pete was pretty animated when we got back together at our motel.

"Guys, we've got to haul it. We have to be at the train station in Hamlet, North Carolina, for a pickup at four o'clock this afternoon. And more than that, we can't go by rental car. We're going to have to make our way by some form of public transportation."

"Then we take the train," I said, and realized how stupid

that was as soon as it came out of my mouth. "No, that won't do, will it? It's too obvious." I tried to think of another way.

"We fly," John announced.

"But it's a simple matter to watch the airports for anybody going to North Carolina today," said Pete. "We'll be picked up."

"We don't take a commercial flight," John countered. "We rent a plane and fly to Hamlet. There's a county airport right outside of town. I flew in there several times when I was getting my private pilot's license after I got back from Vietnam the first time. Then we take the airport courtesy car to the train station.

"From here it should be about a three-hour flight. We just find us a small flight operation at an airfield somewhere around here. Tell 'em we want to rent a plane to fly to North Carolina and that we want one of their pilots to go with us and ferry the plane back. They'll be happy with that and we'll arrive undetected in Hamlet. And with the three of us splitting the cost, it'll also be the cheapest way to go, even paying for the pilot to fly the plane back up here."

"That's brilliant, John," I said. "What kind of a plane should we get?"

"I think a Cessna 182 would be just about perfect. It can carry four people and our luggage. It should be able to make the trip in one jump, and it's relatively fast for a single-engine plane." He picked up the telephone book. "I'll get on the phone and find us one as soon as business hours open. If we can be off the ground by ten o'clock, we should have plenty of time to make it to Hamlet before four o'clock."

I looked at my teammate with admiration. "That's perfect, John. A great idea. While you're arranging it, Pete and I will get the cars turned in and get us checked out of here."

"Sounds good to me," said Pete. "But first, let's go to breakfast. I'm starving."

That, too, was a good idea.

I love flying when I can see something outside, but in those days, I wasn't wild about landing. I was far more accustomed to coming back to earth by parachute.

In the Ranger battalion, I had gone as long as eighteen months at a stretch without landing in an airplane I went up in. It had gotten to the point where I didn't trust any reunion with Mother Earth that I wasn't in control of. John was a good pilot, our trip was uneventful, and the landing was smooth as silk. We said goodbye to the ferry pilot and ambled over to the main hangar and fixed base operator (FBO) to see about arranging transportation into town.

An airport courtesy car was available for our use, but since it was a little over an hour until our pickup time, we elected to have lunch and hang out at the airport before heading into town. Pete struck up a conversation with a young guy who seemed to be the airfield handyman, and he gladly agreed to drive us to the train station.

We arrived at the station with about ten minutes to spare. Just a few seconds past four o'clock, a white van with the appropriate markings pulled to the front of the station and came to a halt. The driver pulled his sunglasses down on the tip of his nose, looked at us over the tops of the lenses, then pushed the glasses back up and adjusted the outside mirror.

That was the "safe" signal. We put our baggage in the back and climbed in. Our instructions had said that the driver would not speak to us, nor were we to speak to him— and it wasn't hard to comply. I'd never met such a quiet person. It was as if the invisible man was driving the vehicle.

We drove down Highway 74 and through the small town of Laurinburg, North Carolina. A few miles outside of town, we turned onto a narrow gravel road that carried us a couple of hundred meters off the highway to a large building that looked like an abandoned trucking company terminal or a warehouse. I looked at the driver as we came to a halt. He returned my look and then very deliberately pointed to a door on the side of the building. I turned to tell my mates to wait in the van while I checked out the building, but the driver motioned for us all to dismount. *The heck with that*, I thought, and told the guys not to let the van leave until I got back.

I got out and tried the door; it was locked. Before I could knock, someone inside threw it open. It was Jerry Knox.

"Come on, Eric. Get your guys and come inside. The driver has a tight schedule to keep."

I waved to Pete and John and motioned for them to hop out. Jerry held the door as we grabbed our stuff and went inside. He then led us down a short corridor, past a few small office cubicles, through another door, and into a large open area the size of a small aircraft hangar. The place was hopping. Trucks were lined up along one wall of the building. Nearby, all of our individual and team equipment was arranged in rows. In the far corner of the bay, an operations center was in place. Guys from the signal section had radios set up, and wires ran out the high windows to the antennas outside.

Jerry sent us to Ron Cardowski for a quick briefing. Ron told us that as part of the play of the culmination exercise, we were responding to an aircraft hijacking. Our OTC class would form the assault troop and field a couple of sniper teams. Ron would be the troop sergeant and Jim Day would be the troop commander. Jim Bush was in charge of the snipers and would run the TOC. The plane, a Boeing 727 full of Americans, was on the ground now at the Laurinburg-Maxton Airport, which for the purposes of the exercise was supposed to be located in a somewhat friendly but very backward and corrupt foreign nation.

Jim Day and a couple of snipers were at the airport now, working with the "local" authorities and trying to sort out a lot of conflicting and confusing information.

Ron told us to check the TOC status board for our team assignments and then move our equipment into the respective team areas we would find laid out on the floor in chalk. I went over to the board for a look at our organization and found my slot.

Assault Troop: C Team
Team Leader: Haney Benevides
Assistant Team Leader: Masters Vandervoort

C Team. That meant that in an assault we would enter over the plane's wings through an emergency exit and move aft. It also meant we would probably form half of the emergency assault team in case things suddenly went bad and we didn't have time to mount a deliberate assault. But if it came to that point, it would be only an attempt to make the best of a bad situation and salvage something from the erupting disaster. Emergency assaults are only executed when terrorists start killing hostages.

This was the first of what would become full-blown hijacked aircraft exercises. During my many years' service in First SFOD-D, I would respond to a couple of dozen actual hijackings and almost the same number of aircraft exercises. But whether it was a real situation or a training exercise, we went at it with the same intensity and sense of urgency. But the training operations were always the more difficult of the two. And that was true of all our training.

About half of the OTC class was already there, so Pete and I found our gear and moved it to our designated team area. Neither Andres nor Jimmy was in yet, so we grabbed their equipment and brought it over too. Then we went to take a look at the information board at the TOC. Not much there yet, just some generalizations about the flight and the estimated number of passengers and some vague information about how many terrorists *might* be aboard. We went back to our team area and got out of the way of the guys at the TOC.

By nightfall, almost everyone was in. We grabbed Jimmy and Andres as soon as they arrived and brought them up to date, which didn't take long because we had so little information. We grabbed ourselves a case of C rations and stepped out onto the loading dock at the back of the building to heat up some supper and compare notes on our experiences over the past few days. Before long, I got a call to report to the TOC for a team leaders' meeting.

Ron had the floor. "We're having difficulties with the local authorities, which is why we haven't moved to the airfield yet, but we've been able to deploy two observation teams around the plane, and we're going to send two emergency assault teams forward just in case things decide to go bad.

"Eric and J.T., your teams will initially comprise the emergency assault. I'll rotate the other teams through that position when we're able to move forward. As soon as we break up here, get everything you need to conduct an assault and also what you'll need to live on for three or four days. Load the stuff in the gray and blue vans and get ready to move to the airport. Don't worry about drivers; I'll provide them. Be ready to move out in ten minutes."

Ron then shifted his attention to the rest of the group. "As for the rest of you, consult the info board. I'll set up a schedule so that everyone will get a chance to work a rotating shift in the TOC. We're going to do our best to get everyone forward under one pretext or the other to at least have a look at the airfield and where the plane is situated.

"There's one final thing." Ron now lowered his voice to a conspiratorial level as he continued. "Jim Day really has his hands full and he needs everybody's help. This exercise alone is a son of a bitch, but whether you know it or not, Jim isn't exactly one of Colonel Beckwith's favorites. If we don't pull this off and do a good job of it, the old man may well use it as an excuse to bounce Jim out of here.

"Officer business is an area I don't generally concern myself with; no NCO does. But Jim Day is one of the best young officers I've ever served with, and I'd like to keep serving with him. I think you all might agree with me when I say that he's a rare breed. He's worth protecting, and we can do that best by making sure he shines. Pass the word to be extra sharp and give Jim every assistance we can—but don't let the other officers know what's going on. They're good guys too, but they're not under the gun right now.

"OK, that's it. You can get back to your teams. J.T., Eric, let me know when you're ready to take off."

So that explains why Jim Day was made commander of the exercise, I thought, *even though he isn't the ranking captain in the class. Ol' Charlie's putting him under the microscope and having a real close look at him. Well, that isn't necessarily bad.*

I agreed with Ron. Jim was a good man, and I wanted to continue working with him. But there was never any danger he would receive less than everyone's utmost and enthusiastic support. That's just the way we operate.

J.T. and I had a quick huddle before we loaded onto the vans for the trip to the airport. We had a couple of things to coordinate in case we got a call en route to immediately execute an emergency assault. We agreed that J.T.'s team would enter over the right wing and clear aft and that my team would enter over the left wing and clear forward. We would run the vans right up to the sides of the airplane and throw the ladders into place, and both teams would mount and enter the plane simultaneously. Speed would have to replace stealth. Once the plane was cleared of terrorists, we would pop all the emergency slides and send the passengers out through every exit. In the event of a fire or an explosion on board, we would open whatever doors we could reach and send people out through those.

Within my team, our order of entry into the plane went like this: The short guys would enter first, Jimmy followed by Andres, and clear down the aisle all the way to the cockpit. I would come in third and Pete would follow me. Since Pete and I were taller than Jimmy and Andres, we would be able to shoot over their heads as they cleared the aisle. Once they hit the forward bulkhead of the cabin, Pete and I would spring forward and clear the cockpit and forward lavatory.

The whole thing sounds tricky, but we knew we could get into the plane and clear our sector as quickly as we could stomp toothpaste from a tube. With our special brand of controlled chaos, we'd enter that plane from the middle and sweep in opposite directions.

We loaded the vans. I got a radio check with the TOC and gave Ron the OK sign, and we were away.

When we arrived at the airfield, we made contact with Jim Day and found a place to set up that was out of sight but within direct access of the taxiway leading to the plane. We never executed an emergency assault, but the preparation for one was always part of the choreography of Delta Force's response to an aircraft hijacking. A few hours later, our whole group moved to the airfield and we rotated the duty of the emergency assault teams.

For the next seventy-two hours, we were put through the wringer. During a hijacking response, one of the things our side does is wage a war of fatigue against the hostage-takers. The objective is to wear them down mentally, physically, and emotionally.

The job of the negotiator is to make sure everything has a price. If the terrorists want water, they have to give something in exchange. If they want the toilets pumped out, they have to give something in return. With every communication, an effort is made to throw the terrorists off their plan and loosen their hold on the initiative. If they can't be induced to give up, we want them to be at their lowest possible state when an assault is mounted. We want them to be tired, frazzled, and drained of confidence. But during this exercise, we were the ones being pushed to the edge.

Deadlines for demands would approach. Tension would build. We would stand-to and get into assault position only to stand-down and pull back. Then, while we were trying to get some rest, some kind of an emergency would come up and we'd stand-to once again. That seemed to happen every few hours.

Jim and Ron had their hands full dealing with the "local authorities" and representatives from the "American embassy," all of whom were actors. The ambassador demanded to be informed of every development in the situation, but instructions came from the National Command Authority in Washington to exclude him. The CIA chief of station (COS) showed up and said that all operational plans had to meet his approval. He was rebuffed and went away mumbling threats. The national minister of internal security demanded that our sniper/observers be pulled in; the U.S. embassy refused to intervene because the ambassador was miffed at being excluded from the information chain. We suspected that the COS had instigated the security minister's demand. Problem after problem arose and had to be dealt with.

The demands were draining to all of us, but particularly to Jim and Ron. During the second day of the ordeal, we grabbed Jim and Ron one at a time, took them to a hidden spot, and made them lie down and rest for a few hours. During those times, we team leaders rotated command duties and took the heat from all the competing interests. We built an invisible force field around our unit to stay focused, adhered to our operational plan, and fought off the worst of the intrusions.

Twice during the second night we prepared to conduct an assault. The first time, we were in approach formation within twenty-five meters of the plane when we were called back. The second time, we were on the plane with our hands on the doors, ready to start the countdown, when we were recalled. That one took a lot of energy out of us, emotionally and tactically. It's a lot more difficult to back down from a target without detection than it is to make the approach in the first place. And every time we pulled back, we had to leave two teams in overwatch in case we were detected and had to launch an emergency assault.

But every difficulty we faced, every problem that surfaced during the course of those exercises would show itself for real over the coming years. And whenever we encountered a new irritant on an operation, we would incorporate it into a future training exercise. Subsequent OTC classes caught the worst of it because they received the accumulated experience of every operation that preceded their arrival.

Finally, just before dawn of the third day, we attacked.

By that point, for everyone involved—the people portraying the hostages, the men portraying the hostage-takers, and us—it felt real. We were all playing for keeps. And when I went through that emergency exit into the plane, I was shooting to kill—it was just a good thing it was blank fire.

What hit me hardest on entering the plane (and what I never got used to, though in the future I was ready for it) was the overwhelming stench. One hundred people crammed into a small space for three days produce an almost unbearable smell. It hits like a blow to the face; it's something we have to physically fight our way through when the doors open. The snipers said that as they closed on the plane to help us handle the passengers, they ran into a wall of foul odor pouring from the open doors as much as fifty meters away.

One other thing was always the same. Whether it was a training exercise or a real operation, if the ordeal had lasted more than twenty-four hours, the hostages and the hostage-takers always reacted the same way. Their sense of reality was restricted to the confines of the plane. The airplane was their planet (in fact, their universe), and everything outside it became alien to them. The group psychology that germinated and took root in that short period of time was always amazing. It's called the Stockholm syndrome, a phenomena in which a hostage comes to identify with his or her captor.

Outside, the hostage handling was taking place according to plan. After the team leaders inside the plane met and talked out an initial report of actions during the assault, we called to Jim Day that we were ready to turn the scene over to the locals. We went through those formalities and climbed off the plane.

We pulled back to the hangar that had been our holding area and stowed our gear. Finally, we were finished. And I, for one, was glad of it. I was so tired I was punchdrunk. Some guys were almost asleep on their feet, and to a man, we were glassy-eyed and weary. Then Ron called us all together.

"We have one thing left to do yet, guys," he told us. "Load all the equipment on the trucks, but keep your pistols and your submachine gun. On the way back, we're going to stop at Range Nineteen and take a shooting test. We have to be there at 0830, so let's get moving. When the equipment is loaded, get on the vans. Team leaders, give me an up when you're ready to move."

I noticed two cadre members, Bill and Carlos, watching us intently as Ron gave us this last-minute information. But there was no complaining as we turned to load the equipment onto the trucks, and after seeing no outbursts, the two observers went to their own vehicle to depart.

Nothing goes unwatched and no action is too small to go unnoted, I thought as I watched Bill and Carlos walk away. We were tired, we were hungry, we were sleepy, and we thought we were finished when they hit us with the news of this next test. And taking one of our shooting tests in this condition was going to be a heck of a challenge.

But as I thought about it, it made perfect sense. The only thing that had not been tested during the assault on the aircraft was our shooting ability. And when we had finally hit the plane, we were tired, hungry, sleepy, and frustrated—all of which would have impacted the accuracy of our shooting. It was imperative that the unit know how each man performed in that condition. Once again, I had to marvel at the thoroughness of our trainers.

I slept all the way back to Fort Bragg, but it seemed that the nap only made me groggier. When we climbed out of the vans at Range Nineteen, Sergeant Major Shumate was there to greet us.

"OK, ladies," he purred. "There's nothing new here this morning; you've all done this drill before. The shooting stations are labeled with your current team designations. Start there and then, as individuals, fill in where you see an opening. Move along with purpose. I don't want to screw around here all morning. And try not to shoot yourselves." He paused. "Unless, of course, it's absolutely necessary." He waved us away with a grin.

I felt as if I was moving in slow motion and had a hangover to boot as I moved to the first point. I usually breezed through these shooting tests, but now it took all my powers of concentration to focus on the required task at each station.

The shooting itself wasn't hard; instinct seemed to take over and guide me. But I had to *think* about what I needed to do and then *tell myself* what I had decided. Fatigue is a powerful narcotic. But the shots went where they were supposed to go, and within the allowed time limits. I didn't realize I was finished until Donny took my scorecard and told me to go sit down.

Finished. Finally finished. Isn't that something? I cleared my weapons and put them in my bag. *It's June now, and I started this ride last September. Not an awfully long time, but a lot has happened since then and I've changed a good bit.*

I had found some things inside myself that had never had a chance to show themselves before. I didn't feel different. I felt, well, *extended*. As if there was now a greater span to my reach. And I felt happy. I had come a long way from the hills of Floyd County, Georgia, in the past ten years. And so far, the value of the trip had been so much greater than the cost.

When everyone was finished, we picked up the spent shells, cleaned the range, and reconvened in the mess hall back at the Ranch for one of "White Water Willie's" fabulous full army breakfasts. We were a hungry bunch and did some serious damage to his menu that morning.

Later, we gathered in the OTC bay for further instructions. Gerhard Altmann spoke with us.

"Gentleman, it is apparent from your current state that it would be senseless to attempt an after-action review of the culmination exercise at this time. Few of you would be able to stay awake, and those who did manage to maintain consciousness I doubt would contribute much to the process. Therefore, let us gather tomorrow morning in this same location and at this same hour. Now take yourselves to a place of rest for some delayed, but well-earned, sleep. I will see you all on the morrow. Until then, I bid you adieu."

Common sense continues to rule, I thought as I gathered my things and walked out to the parking lot. In the Ranger battalion, we always did it by the book and conducted the after-action review immediately following an exercise. We usually gained little from it because we were so dead on our feet it was all anyone could do to stay awake—much less give the review the attention it deserved. The next day, we would all be fresh and mentally alert and able to glean everything possible from a detailed look at the culmination exercise.

I really liked being in a smart organization.

The after-action review lasted seven hours. Each man's actions were gone over in complete detail, and everything that had happened, from the time we'd left Fort Bragg until we'd returned, was brought out and discussed. Mistakes were analyzed and successful methods were noted.

But this was not intended to be the equivalent of a Chinese self-criticism drill. No one was going to be sent back to a reeducation camp. The purpose of the review was to learn everything we possibly could about what we had just done—the good, the bad, and the ugly. We dissected problems and we came up with solutions—and the whole group profited from what we learned.

There is no better way for an organization to improve itself and move forward in a professional manner. But it is a process that must be fundamentally rooted in trust and mutual respect. The instant it becomes a weapon rather than a lens for analysis, the process is dead.

Finally, it was over. OTC-3 had no further business to conduct. Jim Day sent a runner to Colonel Beckwith to let him know we had concluded the review, and the runner returned with a directive that we assemble in the mess hall in fifteen minutes.

The entire unit was gathered in the mess hall when Colonel Beckwith came through the doors with a crash.

"Si'down, si'down." He waved impatiently as he strode

to the center of the room and leaned back against the empty salad bar.

"Well, looks like we got ourselves a bunch of new operators, Country," he said, addressing Sergeant Major Grimes. "Reckon now we gonna have to do sumpthin' with 'em. And it's high time they started earnin' their keep. 'Cause I swear, you boys have been 'bout to eat this unit outta house and home. Now you can start payin' back the cost of your board." He took us all in with a smile that swept the room from side to side.

"Mark this day down in your diaries, men," Beckwith thundered. And then he dropped his voice to a raspy theatrical whisper. "This is the day we've been working towards. This is the day that First Special Forces Operational Detachment–Delta becomes an effective unit. We have now achieved critical mass. By the time we finish business this afternoon, we will be of a size and a configuration that gives us the means of accomplishing the tasks our great nation sets before us.

"Before I leave here today, I'm calling General Shy Meyer, the army chief of staff, and telling him that Delta Force is formed. That Delta Force exists. Then I'm gonna beg him for just three more months to conduct unit training before he tells the joint chiefs we're ready to go. But I'm also going to tell him that if the bell rings tomorrow . . . we can come out fighting."

He turned to the unit adjutant.[2]

"Now, Smith, call out the squadron assignments. And when that's finished, let's have a beer." As he concluded what

[2] The unit adjutant is the officer in charge of administration.

for Colonel Beckwith was a short speech, the mess hall guys wheeled in several beer kegs nestled in trash cans filled with ice.

It was an exciting moment. I felt like a kid at Christmas as I listened to the names being called out and the squadron, troop, and team assignments being made. I had hoped for a posting to a sniper team, but wasn't disappointed in the least when I was called as a member of C Team, Troop One (an assault troop; Troop Two is the sniper troop), B Squadron.

Dave Donaldson had been designated as the leader of C Team, and he waved me over to join him and the other two members of the team. Bill Oswalt was assistant team leader, and the other man was Chris Cable. I had seen Chris on many occasions—he had helped Dave on the range during our demolitions training—but so far, I'd never had the chance to speak with him, though that was about to change.

"Boys, first things first," Dave rumbled around the chaw of tobacco he always kept tucked deep in his jaw. "Let's get at that beer before it's nothing but suds, and then we can talk."

Chris filled four large cups and passed them back to us. We stood close to each other and watched the animated crowd of our friends and comrades. The room rang with laughter and jovial voices, and as I looked around, I realized—*this was a birthday party.*

We were celebrating the birth of our unit. Our conception had happened on paper more than a year before, and since that time, we had undergone a long and difficult gestation. Now a fully grown and reasoning predator, armed with fangs and claws and intelligence, we were able to run and to fight.

We stayed that day and talked with each other long after the beer ran out. It was as if no one wanted to leave. Unconsciously, I guess, we knew that this was a golden day, a day that would never come again, and we were reluctant to let it go.

Now, as I write this, more than a quarter of a century later, I look back on that small place in time and I'm glad to be able to tell myself I was there at the beginning and I know all the heroes who were gathered there, many of whom no longer walk the earth.

It was a rare privilege to be in that room, on that day, with those men. It was an honor to be one of the founding members of that brave band of warriors.

It was an honor and a privilege for which I am eternally thankful.

EPILOGUE

And that was just the beginning. For the next seven years, I served as an operator and a team leader on assault and sniper teams in B Squadron. Our missions carried us around the world, to places such as Iran, Lebanon, the Sudan, Egypt, and throughout Europe, Asia, and much of Latin America. In 1983 we led the invasion of the island of Grenada.

In 1985 I was selected for promotion to the rank of command sergeant major, and in 1986 I departed Delta Force for posting to the U.S. Infantry Brigade stationed in Panama. Following the conclusion of the war in Panama, I retired from the army in the autumn of 1990.

In my postmilitary life, I have negotiated the release of kidnap victims in Colombia and headed the protective details of a Saudi prince, a couple of emirs, and the CEO of the largest corporation in Mexico. In 1994 I was protective detail leader for President Jean-Bertrand Aristide on his return to Haiti.

In between those missions, I conducted antiterrorist operations in Algeria, trained foreign Special Operations forces, foiled a coup attempt, and with my close friends Don and Judy Feeney, conducted the rescues of American children who had been kidnapped and carried overseas.

Sprinkled throughout those activities were a number of surveys, security audits, and opportunities to plan crisis response actions for clients doing business in the more dangerous parts of the globe. As I once responded to a question about why I work the rougher areas of the world, "No one has ever hired me to go to Club Med." And that's the way I like it.

Currently I write and work in the movie and television industry. Periodically I conduct shooting classes for police units around the country, teaching them the shooting skills of the Delta Force operator.

And where has Delta Force been during those years after I departed? The unit moved into its new facility when I left for Panama and immediately worked toward forming a third squadron. That was finally realized as the 1980s came to a close, and it was just in time.

In Panama the boys of Delta ran the dictator General Manuel Noriega to ground and also apprehended a number of his worst henchmen. Afterward they continued their normal activities around the world, with a particular emphasis on Africa. With the outbreak of conflict in the Persian Gulf came missions deep behind the Iraqi lines. They were missions of both reconnaissance and direct action, culminating with hunter/killer strikes on Scud missile positions in the western Iraqi desert, missiles that were targeted against Israel.

Somalia was a rough one. C Squadron and a company of

Rangers were trapped in a Mogadishu neighborhood when their transportation was destroyed and they had to fight for their lives.

In the post-9/11 world, Delta has been in the forefront of the war against Islamic terrorism. They have been heavily engaged in Afghanistan and Iraq while also operating in other, lesser-known areas of the world. Theirs is a war fought in the shadows, far away from news cameras and reporters, and seldom recalled, except by the men who were there. But now and again, when viewing a particular situation on the evening news, I will catch a glimpse of one of the guys. It's always in a bad place, and the Delta Force member is the man who looks like he's at home.

So this was the story of the early days of the world's premier counterterrorism force, an organization that has grown and become even more capable with the passing years. A unit of the United States military that exists for one reason only: the protection of the American people.

In closing, I would like to leave you with this last thought concerning Delta Force and the war on terror: Maintain courage. Have hope. Be patient, but at the same time be vigilant. And remember, we don't call ourselves the Land of the Free and the Home of the Brave for nothing.

Eric L. Haney,
Command Sergeant Major USA (retired)
American Citizen, Soldier

ABOUT**THE**AUTHOR

Eric L. Haney, command sergeant major, USA (ret.), served for more than twenty years in the United States Army's most demanding combat units: as a combat infantryman, as a Ranger, and ultimately as a founding member of Delta Force. In his retirement, he has protected princes, presidents, and CEOs. He has negotiated with Latin American guerrillas for the safe return of hostages, rescued American children kidnapped around the world, and provided security for international oil companies operating in the most dangerous regions on earth. Today he lives and writes in the relative peace and quiet of Marietta, Georgia. This is his first book for young readers.